LONDON ASSOCIATION OF CLASSICAL TEACHERS

LACTOR No. 7

ROMAN
POLITICS

GW00642400

SOURCES FOR THE HISTORY OF THE LATE REPUBLIC

BASED UPON
" ROMAN POLITICS, 80 - 44 B.C."

ROMAN POLITICS

First printed	–	May 1971
Reprinted	–	October 1973
Reprinted	–	December 1975
Reprinted	–	January 1977
Reprinted	–	December 1978
Reprinted	–	September 1982
Reprinted	–	February 1984
Reprinted	–	April 1988
Reprinted	–	October 1991

ISBN 0 903625 09 1

This collection of translated sources for the history of the last years of the republic is based upon <u>Roman Politics,</u> <u>80 - 44 B.C.</u> by J.R. Hawthorn and C. Macdonald, published by Macmillan & Co. Ltd. in 1960. Of the extracts printed there we have omitted the anecdote from Aulus Gellius and the whole of the chapter on 'Caesar and Gaul' and have added the following passages:

> Sallust, <u>Catilinae Coniuratio</u>, 36.4 - 39.4
> Suetonius, <u>Divus Julius</u>, 19
> Cicero, <u>ad Atticum</u>, II, xviii, 1 - 2; VII, xi, 1;
> VIII, xi, 2.

As well as the Latin text of the sources, <u>Roman Politics, 80 -</u> <u>44 B.C.</u> contains valuable notes and introductory material to each chapter, maps, plans, family trees, and a set of excellent indexes; it could thus usefully be read in combination with this LACTOR. We are most grateful to the authors and to the publishers for permission to base this collection upon their book. We are also obliged to the Clarendon Press, Oxford, for permission to use the Oxford Classical Texts of Asconius, Caesar, Cicero, and Suetonius and to Messrs B.G. Teubner, Stuttgart, for permission to use the Bibliotheca Teubneriana text of Sallust.

The following members of the JACT Bureau and the LACT Ancient History group shared the work of translation: P.J. Attenborough, Miss U.M. Bickersteth, J.M. Carter, Miss M. Chandler, N. Chapman, Miss P. Davies, S. Easton, J.T. Hart, B.G. Marchant, P. Matthews, G.R. McMillan, P.L. Moreland, J. Murrell, J.D. Pashley, A.C. Payne, Miss E. Powell, Miss C. Radcliffe, J.A.Smith, C.A. Stray, D.W. Taylor, B.K. Wilson, R.J. Woolfe. For the mistakes that remain, the Glossary, and the introductory notes I am myself responsible.

Emanuel School, S.W. 11   M.A. Thorpe

June, 1970

CONTENTS

GLOSSARY

auctoritas [1]	imperium [4]	servitium [7]
dignitas [2]	dominatio [5]	gratia [8]
otium [3]	regnum [6]	boni [9]

Assembly (Comitia): A meeting of the Roman people as a whole for the purpose of voting either in the elections or on proposed legislation; usually presided over by a consul or praetor. Often preceded by a public meeting (contio), at which speeches were made.

Comitia Centuriata, organized in classes based on a property qualification (census), the richer having an influence disproportionate to their number; its primary function was the election of consuls, praetors, and censors, but it could also act as a legislative assembly.

Comitia Tributa, organized in tribes, the originally geographical groups to which all Roman citizens belonged; its primary function was as a legislative assembly, but it also elected curule aediles, quaestors, and certain lower officers.

Auctoritas [1]: A man influential in public life by reason of family connexions, large clientela, or high office was said to possess auctoritas. The term was typically used of the ex-consuls (consulares) and implied that its possessors could influence even where they could not command. A senatorial resolution vetoed by a tribune was called a senatus auctoritas; it still possessed influence and magistrates might choose to heed it.

Boni [9]: The 'respectable' elements in the state, who could be trusted to defend the status quo. Cf. the Optimates.

Client (cliens) is the term used to denote a free man of inferior status in his relation to one of superior, his Patron (patronus). The two were linked in a bond of mutual obligations, which involved the performance of a range of unspecified but clearly understood acts of service. For example, the client would be expected to support his patron's political interests, and his attendance at his patron's house to greet him in the morning (salutatio) or his presence in his retinue in the forum would serve to illustrate his patron's dignitas. In return, the patron might support his client in the law-courts, with money, or in his own political career. The institution is of fundamental importance in the social and political life of Rome. A prominent Roman's clientela would include not only individuals and groups among the citizen body in Rome or elsewhere in Italy but also provincials.

Colony: In this period, a settlement of Roman citizens, either discharged soldiers or urban poor, in Italy or abroad; self-governing.

Dignitas[2]: "rank, prestige, honour" (Syme); the tribute of public respect for their position claimed by prominent politicians from the people. See Ch. IV.

Dominatio [5], regnum [6]: To describe a man as enjoying or seeking a dominatio or regnum was to claim that he was deliberately flouting the constitutional rights of other citizens and that he aimed at making his position as absolute as that of a master (dominus) over his slaves (servi; hence, servitium [7]) or of a king (rex) over his subjects.

Equestrian Order, Equites: In Cicero's time a citizen class ranking below the Senate. Membership was based upon a property qualification of 400,000 sesterces, though many equites were much richer than this, and the class included the sons of senators before they embarked on the cursus honorum, financiers (publicani, negotiatores), and the ruling classes of the Italian towns (domi nobiles). For their role as jurymen in the quaestiones perpetuae see Ch. II. See P.A. Brunt, The Equites in the Late Republic, reprinted in Seager, The Crisis of the Roman Republic (Heffer, 1969).

Gratia[8]:   Influence, especially in the political field; a man had gratia with those who were obliged to him for some service, E.G. defence in the law-courts.

Imperium[4]:   The supreme administrative and executive power of the Roman state, by virtue of which the senior magistrates - in this period, dictators, masters of the horse, consuls, praetors, proconsuls, propraetors, and the members of certain commissions (E.G. those set up to implement Caesar's Lex Agraria and Lex Campana) - were enabled to carry out their duties.   Deriving probably from the authority enjoyed by the kings of pre-republican Rome, it was originally absolute, and, though subsequent developments (E.G. collegiality, annual magistracies, tribunician veto, the Valerian and Porcian laws, the Lex Villia Annalis) did circumscribe its use by an individual, it remained in essence a power which permitted its holder to do anything not specifically forbidden.

Magistrate: Quaestor: The first step in the cursus honorum (career of public office - the 'promotion ladder' for men in public life); minimum age, 30; Sulla increased the number to 20 annually and made it the qualification for entry to the Senate; elected by the Comitia Tributa Their duties varied, two remaining in Rome to take charge of the Treasury (Aerarium) and most of the others being attached as general assistants to provincial governors.

Aedile: Minimum age, 37; 4 annually - 2 Curule, elected in the Comitia Tributa, and 2 Plebeian, elected in Concilium Plebis.   Their duties included a general supervision of buildings, streets, and market regulations; control of the corn supply (annona); and of the major public games (ludi).   Although the office was not an essential step in the cursus honorum, the comparatively small number of aediles, the ten year gap between quaestorship and praetorship, and the publicity to be won from the presentation of lavish games made it a useful office for an ambitious man.   Ex-aediles sometimes served as iudices quaestionis, presiding over the quaestiones perpetuae.

<u>Praetor</u>: Minimum age, 40; an essential office in the cursus honorum; Sulla increased the number to 8 annually; elected by the Comitia Centuriata. Like the consuls, the praetors possessed <u>imperium</u> and thus, though they were inferior in prestige, they too could, for instance, levy and command armies or summon and preside over the popular assemblies. Their main function, however, in their year of office was judicial; some presided over the quaestiones perpetuae, while the edicts of the senior praetor (<u>praetor urbanus</u>) and his colleagues formed one of the most important sources of Roman law. Thereafter, most praetors left Rome to govern a province.

<u>Consul</u>: Minimum age, 43; 2 annually; elected by the Comitia Centuriata; possessed imperium. The supreme regular magistrates of the republic, their seniority showing above all in their concern with the formation, and not merely the execution, of public policy. Ex-consuls (<u>consulares</u>) might remain active and influential in politics for some time after their year of office - see Ch. IV, and for this and the general state of the Senate after Sulla see J.R. Hawthorn, <u>Greece and Rome</u>, IX, 1 (March 1962).

<u>Municipium</u>: A self-governing Italian town, enjoying in Cicero's day full rights of Roman citizenship.

<u>New Man (novus homo)</u>: The first member of a family to be elected to public office and to enter the Senate; in particular, any such man who became consul. See Ch. IV.

<u>Nobles (nobiles)</u>: Descendants in the male line of a consul.

<u>Optimates</u>: see Ch. IV.

<u>Otium</u>[3]: In a political context, peace within the community, sometimes complementary to peace on the frontiers (pax externa) and contrasted with civil disturbances and revolution (seditio, res novae). See Ch. IV.

<u>Patricians</u>: The aristocracy of birth dominant in the early re-public when they possessed a near monopoly of political power; in Cicero's time they had little except a certain additional prestige and control of a few religious offices.

<u>Patron</u> - see <u>Client.</u>

<u>Plebs</u>, <u>Plebeians</u>: Those not patricians, the great majority
of the Roman people. Possessed their own assembly
(<u>Concilium Plebis</u>) and officers (<u>tribunes</u> - q.v.;
<u>plebeian aediles</u>). See Ch. I.

<u>Populares</u>: see Ch. IV.

<u>Quaestiones Perpetuae</u>: The first quaestio perpetua (standing
court of enquiry) was that for extortion (<u>de rebus
repetundis</u>), established in 149. After Sulla's reforms
there were seven in all, each dealing with a particular
crime; the Sullan scheme included courts for treason
(<u>de maiestate</u>) and electoral bribery (<u>de ambitu</u>), while
one for violence (<u>de vi</u>) was added later. Although each
court had a president (iudex quaestionis - usually a
praetor, sometimes an ex-aedile), his rôle was only
that of a chairman and power lay with the jury, from
whose majority verdict there was no appeal. The
penalties, either capital or monetary, were fixed by
law. On the conflict between senators and equestrians
for control of these courts see Ch. II. Although the
institution of the quaestiones perpetuae had the effect
of greatly reducing the judicial role of the popular
assemblies, it is typically Roman that this was not
abolished by law but remained available as an alternative method of dealing with these crimes; this can be
seen from Caesar's prosecution of Rabirius or from
Cicero's threats to use his power as aedile to impeach
Verres.

<u>Regnum</u> (6) - see <u>Dominatio.</u>

<u>Senatus Consultum Ultimum</u> (SCU): The commonly accepted
title for a decree passed by the Senate in times of great
emergency (also called the s.c. de republica defendun-
da); it instructed the consuls and other magistrates
to ensure the safety of the state (dent operam consules
ne quid detrimenti respublica capiat) and might call
attention to the source from which danger was to be
expected. Like other senatorial decrees it had no
legal force and could not absolve a magistrate from the
provisions of the Valerian and Porcian or Sempronian
laws, though its supporters claimed that such men as

Lepidus in 78 or Catiline in 63 had forfeited their citizen rights and the protection of the laws by their own actions and might reasonably be treated as public enemies (hostes). See Ch. VII, The Exile of Cicero.

Servitium [7] - see Dominatio.

Tribuni Aerarii: Formed one of the three classes from which juries for the quaestiones perpetuae were empanelled between the Lex Aurelia iudiciaria (70) and the Lex Julia iudiciaria (46); in this context they are often classed with the equites against the senators, but their precise status and property qualification are disputed.

Tribunes (Tribuni Plebis), as officers of a section only of the Roman people, were not technically magistrates, but the importance of the office in the political struggles of the late republic made the distinction one with little political significance. Ten tribunes - who had, of course, to be plebeians - were elected annually by the Concilium Plebis; it was not necessary for candidates to have held any office previously, but except in the period between 81 and 75, when Sulla's ban on tribunes being elected to higher office was operating, the tribunate was frequently held by men between their quaestorship and praetorship as an alternative to the aedileship. The tribunes' original rôle was as defenders of the plebs against the patrician magistrates of the early republic; their power to render help to plebeians (ius auxilii) depended on their right of veto (intercessio), which might be exercised against all regular magistrates, other tribunes, elections, laws, and decrees of the Senate, and like the magistrates proper they possessed a power of summary punishment (coercitio) to enable them to enforce their decisions. The ultimate source of their power, however, was the oath taken by the plebeians to protect their inviolability (sacrosanctitas). They also had the right to summon the plebs to meet in the Concilium Plebis, whose decree (plebiscita) had since 287 possessed the same validity over the whole people as laws passed in the popular assemblies, and were entitled to attend, and even summon, meetings of the Senate. For the tribunate in the 70's see Ch. I.

THE TRIBUNATE

Whatever Sulla's motives may have been in restricting the rights and powers of the tribunes, and whatever other consequences his law may have had, it was upon this point that the populares of the 70's concentrated the force of their attack on the Sullan system. If the speech which Sallust puts into the mouth of Macer can be taken as evidence for the political situation in the 70's, and not simply for the conventions which a Roman historian followed when writing a 'tribune's harangue to the people', it clearly indicates that there was a long tradition of plebeian support for the tribunate as a defence against the arbitrary power of the nobles. Moreover, the tone of various references in it - to the patricians, the secessions, the capture of the consulate by the plebeians - suggest that certain strands in the tradition had originated when the struggle between the Orders was at its height and still had sufficient emotional force over two hundred years later to be worth exploiting by an anti-Sullan tribune. The absorption of leading plebeians into the political establishment and the consequent change from an aristocracy of birth (patricians) to one of office (nobiles) must have left many of the plebeians' grievances unsatisfied; they had changed only their masters.

C. Licinius Macer, tribune in 73, wrote a history of Rome with an anti-senatorial bias; he became praetor, probably in 68, and in 66 was convicted in the extortion court.

For the propaganda of the Optimates see Ch.IV (Cicero, pro Sestio, 96 - 105).

Sallust, Histories, fr III, 48.

The Speech of the Tribune Macer to the Plebs.

1.   Citizens of Rome, you are perfectly well aware of the difference between the rights bequeathed to you by your ancestors and this state of slavery[7] engineered

by Sulla. I need not, therefore, remind you at length of the many occasions when the plebs took up arms and seceded from the patricians, of the wrongs which led them to this course, nor of how they created the tribunes of the plebs to safeguard all their rights.

2. I have now only to encourage you and to set out at your head upon the path by which I believe we must regain

3. our liberty. I have not overlooked the vast resources of the nobility whose domination [5] I seek to overthrow, single-handed and powerless, clad in but the empty illusion of a magistracy. I know too how much safer it is to ally oneself with companions in crime

4. than to stand upright alone. But apart from the hope I have in you, which outweighs my fear, it is my conviction that it is better for a brave man to fight for liberty, and lose, than never to have fought at all.

5. Yet all others who have been elected to champion your rights have turned the whole force of their authority[4] against you, induced by favour [8] or expectation or reward to do so. They think it better to do wrong

6. for profit than to act rightly without it. And so they have all become the slaves[5] of a minority, who have used the pretext of war to seize control of treasury, armies, kingdoms[6] , and provinces. They have made themselves a stronghold from the spoils they have taken from you, while despite your numbers you offer yourselves to these few individuals like cattle to be owned and used, stripped of everything your forefathers left you - except, of course, that you exercise your votes to choose your masters[5] where once you

7. chose your protectors. And so they have all gone over to the side of the nobility, whereas, if you will only take back what is yours, the great majority will rejoin you. Few there are who have the spirit to fight for what they value; the rest obey the stronger.

8. You must surely realize that there is no obstacle on earth that can stop you if you work together. Even when you are apathetic and idle, they fear you. Do you imagine that Gaius Cotta, a consul from the heart of the ruling clique, had any other motive than fear for restoring a few of the rights of the tribunes of the plebs? Certainly when Lucius Sicinius spoke out

2

about the tribunician powers, - and he was the first to dare to -, you hardly raised your voices, and he was suppressed; but the nobles learnt to fear your anger before you came to resent your wrongs. I cannot find words for my astonishment at your patience, citizens of Rome; for you had come to understand that all hope

9. was vain. When Sulla, who had forced you into this appalling servitude[7], died, you thought your troubles were at an end: but no, there came Catulus, far more

10. savage. The consulship of Brutus and Mamercus was interrupted by insurrection. Then Gaius Curio played the despot[5] to the extent of putting an innocent tribune

11. to death. Last year you witnessed the ferocity with which Lucullus attacked Lucius Quintius. Finally, look at the turmoil now being stirred up against me! Yet this activity will certainly turn out to have been futile, if there is any likelihood of their giving up their tyranny[5] before you break free of your slavery[7]; especially since in this struggle of citizen with citizen many claims are made, but what both sides are really

12. fighting for is to lord it[5] over you. Other matters have flared up from time to time, arising from greed or hatred or indiscipline; only one thing has remained constant, which has been coveted by both sides and has been snatched away for all time: the tribune's power, the weapon that our ancestors fashioned in defence of

13. their freedom. I advise you, indeed I beg you, to take good heed of this: do not alter the names of things merely to suit your own feebleness; do not christen slavery[7] 'peace'[3]. Nor is there any possibility of enjoying this 'peace'[3], if wickedness overcomes truth and honesty; you would still have had it, if you had remained entirely passive. They are on their guard now, and if you do not triumph they will repress you more terribly, since wrongdoing always finds safety in excess.

14. What are my recommendations then? First of all, you must abandon your present manner of behaviour: your tongues are quick, but you have little fire in your hearts and you forget liberty the moment you come away

15. from a meeting. And what are you waiting for? Surely I do not need to remind you that your ancestors acted like men, winning the right to elect tribunes of the

plebs and to stand for the consulship - an office previously confined to patricians - and freeing the decisions
of the plebs from patrician veto.   All power lies in your
hands, and, whereas you now weakly accept orders that
profit others, you could quite easily judge by your own
interests whether to carry them out or not.   Do you
imagine that Jupiter or some other god will come down

16.   to advise you?   It is you who give force to the great
powers[4] of the consuls and the decrees of the senate -
by obeying them, and you hasten of your own accord to
further and increase the unbridled power they hold over

17.   you.   I am not urging you to take revenge for your
wrongs, but simply to long for some rest from them;
nor is it because I desire trouble, as they complain,
but because I wish to end it, that I seek restitution
according to universal law;   and if they persist in with-
holding it, I recommend neither a resort to arms, nor
a secession, but only that you cease to volunteer your

18.   lives.   Let them have their commands[4] and exercise
them[4] as they like;   let them hunt triumphs and pursue
Mithridates, Sertorius, and the remnants of the exiles,
and let them take their family portraits with them: but,
let those who have no share of the fruits be spared the

19.   toil and the danger.   Unless, of course, that hastily
carried corn law is the reward for your services.
According to this, they think five bushels each a month
is the price of your liberty - no more than prison rations;
for just as these scanty rations keep prisoners from
death but sap their strength, so this small dole offers
no release from family cares and does not even begin to

20.   satisfy the hopes of the idlers.   But even if the allowance
were generous, it is offered as the price of slavery[7];
what apathy it would be to be deceived like this and
willingly to give thanks for the misuse of your own pro-

21.   perty!   Do not let them trick you.   For there is no
other means by which they can prevail against you all,
nor will they try.   And so they prepare palliatives and
put you off until Gnaeus Pompeius arrives.   Yet see how
they treat him: they raised him on high, when they
feared Sertorius;   he soon released them from their fear,

22.   and they reward him with savage attacks.   And these
self-proclaimed champions of liberty, many as they are,
are not ashamed to wait for one man before they have the
courage to redress a wrong or the power to defend a

23. right. For me anyway the evidence is sufficient that young Pompeius, who has won such glory, prefers to be the leading man in the state with your support than to be an associate of theirs in despotism[5] and that he will take the lead in restoring the powers of the tribunes.

24. But in earlier days, citizens of Rome, each of you found protection in many others, not all of you in one man. In those days no one person had it in his power to grant or take away anything of such importance.

25. I have said enough; and it is not inadequate know-
26. ledge that brings me to a stop. You are in the grip of some apathy; neither glory nor outrage stirs you; in your present sloth you see everything differently, and think you have freedom and to spare, merely because your backs do not feel the rod and you are allowed to come and go as you please, by the kindness of your
27. rich masters. As for the country folk, they have none of these privileges, but are slaughtered in the quarrels of the powerful and are sent off to the provinces like
28. gifts to the magistrates. Thus there is battle, and victory for the few; the plebs, whatever happens, are treated as the conquered – and this will be truer every day, if the efforts of the oligarchy to retain their mastery[5] are greater than yours to regain your freedom.

THE EQUESTRIANS AND THE LAW COURTS

In 149 the Lex Calpurnia established a standing court of civil enquiry to deal with cases of extortion by provincial governors, the quaestio perpetua de rebus repetundis. Its jurors were at first senators, but in 122 the Lex Acilia transferred control of the courts to the equites, and apart from a brief interval of mixed senatorial and equestrian juries (106 - 104) they retained control until 82 when Sulla restored the courts, of which there were by then seven, to the Senate.

The quaestiones played an important part in the politics of the late republic and this was particularly true of the extortion court, as most of the cases brought before it concerned crimes committed by a magistrate when on an official tour of duty in the provinces; the prosecutor could easily pass from an attack on the individual magistrate to one on the system under which such men could be elected, the iniquity of their supporters, and the corruption of the governing class in general. For a young man with political ambitions the first step was often to win a reputation in the courts, either by prosecution as Caesar seems to have preferred - a dangerous course as one might make enemies, or - more cautiously - in defence work, as Cicero had hitherto preferred.

Several notorious cases in the extortion court had recently seemed to indicate that senatorial juries were unduly reluctant to convict their fellows. In 77 Caesar prosecuted Dolabella (cos 81); he was defended by Hortensius and acquitted. In 76 C. Antonius (cos 63) was accused by Caesar and acquitted. In 74 Terentius Varro was accused, and again Hortensius secured an acquittal - this was the case of the coloured voting tablets. Hence the strong popular approval for Pompey's promise to deal with the situation. Thus, when in 70 the Sicilians appealed to Cicero to prosecute Verres on their behalf, he accepted willingly; it was an ideal case, with none of the risks prosecution usually involved. The evident corruption of senatorial juries and the strong Metellan backing for Verres could serve as an excuse for Cicero in the event of an acquittal - and Hortensius was again acting for the defence; while in the event of Verres' conviction they would merely increase his success in the eyes of the people.

Cicero, I in Verrem, 35 - 47

35.   But as things stand, Hortensius, since you take so much pleasure in the despotic power [5, 6,] you now enjoy over our courts of law, and since there exist men who seem almost deliberately to court the hatred and ill-will of the Roman people and who feel no shame at their outrageous behaviour and the ill-repute it brings them but rather wish it to continue, I declare publicly that, though the task I have undertaken may well be difficult and dangerous, I still consider it to be one to which I may properly devote all the

36. resources of my age and energy.   The whole senatorial order is suffering from the unprincipled and unscrupulous conduct of a small minority and is crushed by its poor reputation in the law courts.   I therefore declare publicly that I shall attack these men; my hostility to them will be bitter, implacable, and unremitting.   This is the task which I claim as mine by right, to which I shall devote myself when aedile, - a fitting task, indeed, for the position of trust to which the Roman people has appointed me from 1st January, signifying thereby its wish for me to guide its deliberations about affairs of state and the treatment of wicked and criminal men.   This is the spectacle which I promise to the Roman people as the fairest and finest of my aedileship.   Here is advance notice of my intention.   I advise all those who have made a practice of employing bribery to pervert the course of justice, - all who have offered or contributed money, have accepted money, or have acted as agents or go-betweens in any way - to heed it carefully; their backers too, men who have unscrupulously lent their support to this process.   I warn these foul criminals not

37. to meddle in this trial, not even to think of doing so.   Next year Hortensius will be consul, enjoying supreme command[4] and power: I shall be aedile, little more than a private citizen.   Yet the promise I now make is of such significance and its fulfilment will be so welcome to the Roman people that the consul himself when matched against me on this issue shall seem of less importance - if this is possible - than a private citizen.

I shall bring to your notice, in full and incontrovertible detail, the whole story of the disgraceful crimes committed in the courts during the ten years since control of
38. the juries was transferred to the Senate. I shall inform the Roman people of the fact that for the period of equestrian control of the courts, for an unbroken period of almost fifty years, there was not one case, jurors, not a single case in which the faintest suspicion attached to any member of the equestrian order that his verdict had been influenced by receipt of a bribe; but that, once the Senate recovered control of the courts and the power of the Roman people over individual senators was removed, Quintus Calidius declared when found guilty that a man of praetorian rank could not decently be convicted for less than three million sesterces; that, when Quintus Hortensius was praetor in charge of the extortion court, the damages assessed after the conviction of the senator Publius Septimius included a sum to cover
39. his receipt of bribes when serving as a juror. Nor are these the only cases. It was established beyond any possibility of doubt that Caius Herennius and Caius Popilius, two senators convicted of misappropriating public funds, and Marcus Atilius, who was convicted of treason, had all accepted bribes while serving as jurors. Again, when Caius Verres was urban praetor and was organizing the system by which jurors are allotted to courts, it came to light that certain senators voted against a defendant whose case they had not heard and thus secured his conviction and that one particular senator who was serving as a juror accepted money both from the defendant for distribution on his behalf to the other jurors and also, in the very same case, from
40. the prosecutor to vote against the defendant. And what of that notorious case in which the verdicts of the jurors who were under oath were recorded on tablets of different coloured wax? How can I find words to express my horror that this should happen in Rome and with a jury of senators? It is a disgraceful and damaging stain upon the honour of the entire senatorial order. These crimes will, I assure you, all receive my most strict and careful attention.

You can imagine then what my attitude will be if I have reason to believe that any such offence has been committed in this case. What makes me particularly suspicious - and I can produce many witnesses to the truth of this statement - is something Caius Verres was frequently heard to say in

Sicily in the presence of many people. He used to claim that he would never be convicted of plundering his province as he had a promise of support from a powerful friend; he was not making money just for himself, but had so planned his three years' governorship of Sicily that he would think he was doing very nicely if he could put one year's profit in his own pocket, could hand over the second year's to his patrons and the men who were to defend him in the courts, and could keep back the entire profit of his third year, the richest and most lucrative of

41. all, for distribution as bribes to his jurors. This prompts me to repeat a remark which I made recently before Manlius Glabrio while exercising my right to reject jurors and which, I understand, made a great impression on the Roman people. I said that I thought a time would come when our foreign subjects would send deputations to Rome to request the repeal of the extortion law and the abolition of the court concerned with this offence. The provincials think, you see, that if the courts were abolished, each governor would extort from them only so much as he considered sufficient for his own use and his children's; whereas now, with the courts in the state they are, each governor takes enough to satisfy himself, his patrons, his advocates, the praetor who presides over his trial, and his jurors – there is no end to it, in fact. They believe they could satisfy the demands of the most rapacious of governors but that they are totally unable to pay the sum necessary to ensure the acquittal of a man whose guilt is beyond doubt.

42. What a tribute this is to our legal system ! What a splendid reputation we senators enjoy ! Our allies want to abolish the extortion court, which our ancestors established to protect them ! Do you imagine that Verres would ever have felt so confident about the outcome of this trial if he didn't share this low opinion of you? You have greater reason to hate him – if this is possible – than the rest of the Roman people, for he clearly considers you as rapacious, as wicked, and as corrupt as himself.

43. In the name of the gods, jurors, do not neglect this situation. Think how it may develop. I warn you publicly that in my opinion this opportunity to free the whole senatorial order from the unpopularity and disgrace under which it now labours has been given you by the gods. You must not refuse it. Nobody believes any longer in the strict impartiality of our legal system or its freedom from corruption; its very existence has come to seem a farce.

And so, we are despised by the Roman people and held in contempt, crushed by the weight of a scandal that has too

44. long continued. This too was the only reason why the Roman people was so keen to see the tribunes enjoy their full powers once more. Yet the restoration of tribunician power was only the ostensible object of its demands: what it really wanted was to recover control of the courts. The wise and distinguished Quintus Catulus realized this. When he was asked his opinion in the debate on Pompey's motion that the power of the tribunes should be restored he began by declaring with the full weight of his authority [1] that the senators were exercising their control of the courts in an inefficient and immoral way. He pointed out that if the senators serving in the courts had been prepared to meet the expectations of the Roman people, the loss of tribunician

45. power would never have been felt so keenly. Again, when Pompey himself made his first public speech as consul-elect, outside the city, and declared - as was generally expected - that he would restore the power of the tribunes, one could hear an encouraging murmur of approval from the crowd. But when he went on to say in that same speech that the provinces had been ravaged and plundered by their governors, that the courts were an offence against morality and justice alike, and that he intended to deal with the situation, - then it was not just a murmur: a full-throated roar showed that this was what the Roman people really

46. wanted. The eyes of the world are now upon you. Each and every one of you is being watched, to see how well he keeps his juror's oath and how effectively he protects our laws. Men see that since the tribunician law was passed one senator has so far been convicted, a man of very modest resources, and though they find nothing to criticize in his conviction, nothing has yet occurred to arouse their great enthusiasm. After all, there is nothing praiseworthy about a spotless conscience when nobody has the means or the

47. inclination to corrupt it. In this trial you will judge the accused, the Roman people will judge you. This is the case which will decide whether senators will ever convict a wealthy man even when his guilt is clear. Verres is remarkable for only two qualities - the magnitude of his crimes and the depth of his pocket: if he is acquitted, men must needs suspect the worst; influence [8], family ties, good deeds on other occasions, a spot of grey to break the uniform black of his sins - none of these will seem sufficient reason to acquit a man guilty of so many monstrous crimes.

III

POMPEY AND THE TRIBUNATE

In 67, the tribune A. Gabinius had passed a law giving Pompey a command with wide powers against the pirates. Another tribune, C. Cornelius, who had previously been Pompey's quaestor in Spain, had passed laws restricting the Senate's right to grant privilegia (exemptions for particular individuals from existing laws) and insisting that praetors should administer justice in accordance with their edicts; he had also proposed other administrative measures which were not passed. In 66, the tribune C. Manilius brought forward a bill entrusting Pompey with command of the war against Mithridates, and despite fierce resistance from the Optimates his proposal became law. Cicero, who was praetor in charge of the extortion court in this year, spoke for the bill - his first purely political speech. Towards the end of 66 the Optimates prosecuted Manilius for extortion and, when this case lapsed at the end of the year, attacked him in the treason (maiestas) court in 65. Cornelius was prosecuted in the maiestas court in 66 and again in 65.

The objection to Gabinius' serving as legate to Pompey in the campaign against the pirates was based upon the Lex Licinia et Aebutia (mid-second century), which forbade any man to hold office under the terms of a law he had himself proposed, and Cicero's treatment of the matter, with its reference to other tribunes who had become legates, is somewhat disingenuous. There was, of course, no legal objection to his serving in this capacity under the Manilian law.

Cicero, **de imperio Cn. Pompei, 51-64**

51.   I know that opposition to this view comes from a most distinguished man, and one devoted to Rome - Quintus Catulus, who has received the highest marks of your favour; and also from Quintus Hortensius, a man endowed with the highest gifts of position and fortune, of virtue and character. I admit that you have often attached great importance to the influence and prestige[1] of these men, and this is

as it should be. In this case, as you are well aware, their influence and prestige[1] are set against me; but, although they are men of great eminence, we must disregard their views[1], for we can reach the truth simply by considering the facts. All the more easily indeed, because the truth of all my previous statements is admitted by my opponents; they admit that this is a great and unavoidable war and that Pompey is the one man who has all

52. the highest qualifications. So what is Hortensius saying? He admits that if the whole command is to be entrusted to one man, the most deserving candidate is Pompey; but he denies that the command should go to one man. But this is an argument which is already out of date. It is the facts, not mere words, which have refuted it. You yourself, Quintus Hortensius, used all the force of your unique eloquence to make a weighty and brilliant speech in the Senate against that determined man Aulus Gabinius, when he had introduced a law in favour of the appointment of a single commander against the pirates; you also spoke from this very platform, and at great length, against the same measure.

53.   But consider: if your influence had carried more weight on that occasion than the safety and true interests of the Roman people, should we today be enjoying our present renown and an empire[4] covering the world? Did you think that we had an empire[4] then, when our legates, quaestors, and praetors were being captured, when we were unable to receive supplies - either official or private - from any of our provinces, and when the seas were so completely closed to us that we could conduct neither our personal nor our public business overseas?

54.   Has there ever before been a state so fragile or so tiny that it could not defend its own harbours, its territory, and at least some part of the surrounding countryside or coast by its own efforts? And I am not thinking about important states such as Athens, which is reported to have had extensive control of the sea at one time, nor of Carthage, which was a great maritime power, nor Rhodes, whose naval skill and renown has survived to our own times; has any state ever been in this position? Yet for a number of years before the law of Gabinius this great people of Rome, which kept a name for invincibility in naval affairs right up to our own day, was actually

deprived of a large part - indeed much the largest part - not simply of its resources, but even of its status[2] as an imperial power[4].

55.   Our ancestors defeated King Antiochus and Perses at sea and overcame the Carthaginians in every sea-battle despite their unequalled experience and excellent equipment; we could not match up to the pirates on a single occasion. In former times we could keep Italy secure and also guarantee the safety of all our allies right to the ends of the earth by the prestige[1] of our power[4].   In those days the island of Delos, set so far from Rome in the Aegean Sea, was frequented by traders and merchants from all over the world; it was packed with wealth, tiny, and defenceless - yet it had no fear.   Yet we ourselves were not only kept out of our provinces, the coast of Italy, and our own harbours, but were actually denied the use of the Appian Way! In times like these, would any Roman magistrate not have been ashamed to climb this platform which our ancestors had left to us adorned with sea-trophies and the spoils of

56. captured fleets? On this occasion the Roman people realized that you and the others who were of your opinion were expressing your sentiments with the best of intentions. But all the same, when it was a question of the safety of the state, this same Roman people preferred to pay attention to their own affliction than to the weight of your opinion[1]. As a result, a single law, a single man, a single year set you free from that distress and humiliation; what is more, it created a situation where it would once more really seem that you held sway over all nations and peoples, by land and by sea.

57.   So it seems to me even more shameful that objections have been raised to the appointment of Gabinius as one of Pompey's lieutenants, when Pompey himself has asked for this and in fact insisted on it - though whether this objection is directed against Pompey or against Gabinius or (as is more probable) against both together I do not know. Can it really be that a general who is requesting the lieutenant of his choice for a war of such importance is not entitled to obtain his request? Yet others, whose only purpose has been to rob our allies and plunder our provinces, have secured the deputies of their own choice. Or that the very man by whose law the safety and honour[2] of the Roman people and all nations have been established should have no

share in the success of the general and of the army which has been set up on his advice and at some personal risk?

58. Now Caius Falcidius, Quintus Metellus, Quintus Caelius Latiniensis, Cnaeus Lentulus - all of whom I mention with respect - were all able to secure appointment as general's lieutenant in the year after holding the office of tribune of the plebs. Is this fastidiousness to apply only in the case of Gabinius? The war is being conducted under the law which he introduced and by a general and an army which he created through your votes. Surely he was entitled to special consideration? I hope that the consuls will refer the question of his appointment to the Senate. If they hesitate or make difficulties, I promise to refer it myself. I shall not be put off by the hostility of any magistrate, but relying on your support shall defend your right to appoint whomever you wish to this position. I shall not tolerate any interference except the tribunician veto - and those who threaten this will, I think, consider carefully the limits of their power. In fact, in my opinion, citizens, Aulus Gabinius is the only man who deserves to be associated with Pompey in the victories of this naval war, in that Gabinius, with your support, was responsible for entrusting the war to a single commander, while Pompey, once he was given command and had undertaken the war, brought it to its conclusion.

59. It still seems to me to be necessary to say something about the viewpoint which is backed by Quintus Catulus' authority[1]. He wanted to know what would happen if you placed full power in Pompey's hands and anything happened to him; on whom would you rely then? Then he received a great tribute to his own character and standing[2] when you virtually unanimously said that you would rely on him. Now certainly he is a man of such quality that there is no enterprise so great or difficult that he could not guide it by his wisdom, supervise it with his integrity, and bring it to completion by his ability. Yet in this one case I am in complete disagreement with him; for as mankind's existence is fickle and fleeting, so the state is the more bound to take advantage of the career and character of a genius,

60. for as long as heaven allows. Now Catulus protests that we should not allow innovations which contravene the established precedents of our ancestors. This is not the place for me to point out that our ancestors were always guided by tradition in peacetime, but that in war they followed expediency, constantly adapting their policies to the new

circumstances of new emergencies; nor to say that two
wars of the greatest importance - against Carthage and
in Spain - were successfully terminated by one commander,
and that two most powerful cities - Carthage and Numantia -
which constituted a very serious threat to our empire[4],
were both destroyed by the same man - Scipio. I shall
not relate how, in recent times, you and your fathers
decided that the hopes of the Roman Empire [4] should be
vested in Caius Marius, so that this one man controlled
the wars against Jugurtha, against the Cimbri, and against
the Teutones. But consider the case of Cnaeus Pompeius,
for whom Quintus Catulus does not want any new precedent
to be established; consider what a number of innovations
have already been introduced in his case, and with the full
backing of Catulus.

61.   What could be so unprecedented as that a young man,
holding no office, should raise an army at a time of crisis
in the state? But he raised one. Or that he should command it? Yet he commanded it. Or that his command
should be crowned with success? But it was. What could
be so opposed to custom as that the command[4] of an army
should be given to a young man far below the minimum age
even for admission to the Senate, that Sicily and Africa
should be entrusted to his control and the conduct of the
war in that province? But in these provinces he acted
with outstanding integrity, dignity, and ability; he brought
to an end a serious war in Africa, and led his army home
in victory. What could be so unheard of as for a Roman
eques to celebrate a triumph? Yet the Roman people not
only saw this event, but every citizen clearly thought he
should attend it and should join in the celebrations with
62. enthusiasm. What could be so novel as that, when there
were two excellent and resolute consuls, an eques should
be sent with consular power to a grave and formidable war?
Yet he was sent. In fact, though there were at that time a
number in the Senate who argued that a private individual
should not be sent with the power of a consul, Lucius
Philippus is reported as having said that in his opinion
Pompey should be sent 'not in place of one consul, but in
place of both'. In fact he gave rise to such expectations
of success that the official duties of both consuls were put
into the hands of one young man with talent. What could
be more extraordinary than that, exempted from the laws
by a senatorial decree, he should be made consul before

15

he was legally allowed to hold any magistracy at all ? What could be more incredible than that while still an eques he should be entitled by decree of the Senate to hold a second triumph? All the innovations made in individual cases from the beginning of our history are fewer than those we have witnessed in the case of this single man.

63. And all these remarkable and revolutionary precedents have been established for Pompey by the influence[1] of Quintus Catulus and other distinguished men of similar status [2].

So long as the influence [1] of these men was exerted in support of Pompey's merits[2], it always met with your approval. They should, therefore, be careful that their present objection to your plans for Pompey - to the verdict[1], that is, of the Roman people - should not seem intolerably unjust. This is especially the case now, since your choice of Pompey as the only man fit to command in the war against the pirates, a choice made despite their opposition, fully entitles the Roman people to defend its

64. verdict[1] in his case against any possible objection. Now if on this occasion you acted unwisely, with too little attention to the interests of Rome, then these men are right to try to temper your zeal with their good sense. But, if it was you who then showed the greater patriotic insight and you who, despite their resistance, by your own actions brought prestige[2] to this empire[4] of ours and safety to the whole world, then these leading men ought surely now to concede that they and others must bow to the unanimous authority[1] of the Roman people.

Asconius, in Cornelianam, pp. 59 - 62C

Q. Asconius Pedianus (9 BC - AD 76) was a scholar who wrote a commentary upon Cicero's speeches; particularly when, as in the case of the pro Cornelio, the speech itself is no longer extant, Asconius provides us with such historical evidence which we should not otherwise possess.

52. The following year in the consulship of M'Lepidus and L. Volcacius - the year in which Cicero was praetor - the brothers Cominius brought Cornelius to trial under a law of the dictator Sulla dealing with treason. Publius brought the accusation and Caius supported it. P. Cassius

instructed Cominius to attend on the tenth day, as was the
custom, but failed to put in an appearance that day himself,
either because he had been called away on some business
connected with the corn supply or simply because he was
doing the defendant a favour, and Cornelius' accusers were
surrounded in front of the tribunal by well-known gang
leaders.   They were threatened with death, if they did not
abandon the case soon.   Indeed they barely escaped this
fate through the arrival of the consuls who had come to
lend their support to the defendant.   Thereupon the Cominii fled up some stairs and lay there in hiding till nightfall:
then they made their way over the roofs of the neighbouring
houses and so out of the city.   On the next day, when P.
Cassius had taken his seat, the accusers were called but
were found to be absent and the case against Cornelius was
dropped.   The two Cominii, however, were involved in a
great scandal on the allegation that they had sold their
silence for a great sum of money.

53.   Then in the following year in the consulship of L.
Cotta and L. Torquatus - the year in which this speech was
delivered by Cicero just after he had completed his praetorship - Manilius, who had organized the gang leaders to
break up the trial of Cornelius, was himself accused.   In
accordance with a decree of the Senate both consuls were
presiding over this trial, and because of this, Manilius did
not answer the charge and was condemned.   Thereupon
Cominius made a reappearance to clear himself of the slan-
der that he had taken a bribe and he again prosecuted Cornelius for a constitutional offence.   The case was heard in
an atmosphere of great expectation.   Cornelius, however,
who was shocked by the fate of Manilius, brought only a
few of his friends into court so as not even to give Cominius'
supporters a chance to shout.

        There gave evidence against him the leading men of
the state, men who had very great influence in the senate,
Q. Hortensius, Q. Catulus, Q. Metellus Pius, M. Lucullus,
M'Lepidus.   Their testimony was that they had seen Cornelius perpetrate an apparently unprecedented act in his
tribunate when despite a veto he actually read his bill himself in front of the rostra. Their aim was to make it appear
that they considered this action to be tantamount to a charge
of treason;   for the right of veto was practically removed,
if tribunes were allowed to act like this.   Cicero could not

17

deny that this had happened but was reduced to saying that the mere fact of a tribune reading a bill himself did not entail an attack on the constitutional powers of a tribune. Indeed if you read the speech, you will discover the thorough mastery of the theoretical and practical sides of oratory which Cicero showed in delivering it. For he avoided affronting the prestige[2] of those outstanding citizens against whom he was speaking, whilst at the same time not letting his client suffer because of their influence[1]. Also apparent will be the moderation he used in handling a matter which would have been so difficult for a man of lesser ability.

54. He had, however, on his side the fact that, as I have said, Cornelius, - apart from the fact that he was known to be openly opposed to the wishes of the leading men, - had done nothing in the rest of his career which could be greatly censured. Moreover, Globulus himself, who had interposed the veto on that occasion, supported Cornelius, and - another point that I have mentioned before - the fact that Cornelius had been a quaestor of Pompeius Magnus was to his advantage with two sections of the jury, the equites Romani and the tribuni aerarii. It also carried weight with the majority of the senators who formed the third section, apart from those who were connected with the leading families. The case was heard with a large audience and amid great speculation as to what the verdict would be.... Those present noted that evidence was being given by most distinguished citizens and that the defendant was admitting what they said. There survives the speech of the accuser Cominius, which is well worth the trouble of reading, not only because we have the speeches of Cicero in defence of Cornelius, but also for its own sake. Cicero, as he himself points out, spoke in Cornelius' defence for a period of four days; it appears that he abridged all these proceedings and published them in two speeches. Q. Gallius the praetor was in charge of this trial.

IV

OPTIMATES AND POPULARES

These terms belong originally to the world
of propaganda and, like many political labels, say
more about how the groups to which they are applied saw themselves and hoped to be seen by others
than about what they actually were. (Cf. Labour,
Christian Democrats, Progressives, etc.) Neither
group had any formal organization or list of members, but the criteria for calling a man an optimate
or a popularis - though they might vary slightly
with occasion or speaker - were sufficiently constant and sufficiently well-understood to justify
the use of the labels for most of this period.
Fundamentally they were criteria of political method
or temperament and not, as might be the case today,
of ideology. The Optimates were those who defended the established traditions of political life because
they found it possible to realize their ambitions
within them; in particular, they attached great
importance to the rôle of the Senate and within it to
that of a small group of leading men (principes),
usually ex-consuls (consulares), whose political
influence (auctoritas) would ensure the success of
their plans. The Populares were those who preferred instead to work through the only alternative
non-military source of political power in Rome, the
popular assemblies.

An important consequence follows from this
basic difference. The Optimates were a coherent
and more or less permanent group, whose members
were closely linked by social, and even family,
relationships; they met regularly in the Senate, and
these meetings provided their leaders with an opportunity to test opinion, to deploy their influence, and
to mobilize the political energies of their supporters.
The leaders of the Populares could not count on any
of these advantages. They had first to create
popular support for their actions and thus found themselves virtually committed to specific policies which
would achieve this effect. These were almost always
opposed by the Optimates, and, while the immediate

effect of these clashes may have benefitted the
Populares in providing them with a focus for their
political loyalties, the long-term effect – particularly in combination with the problems caused by
the large-scale provincial commands of Pompey
and Caesar – was so to raise the temperature of
politics in Rome that by the end of the 50's the
division between Optimates and Populares has
become quite inadequate as the basis for an analy-
sis of Roman politics.

Cicero, pro Sestio, 96 – 105.

As quaestor in 63 P. Sestius had vigorously
supported Cicero's policy against the Catilinarians
and in 57 as tribune he had been active in securing
his recall from exile. Thus, when in 56 he was
prosecuted by Clodius for violence (vis), Cicero
gladly undertook his defence. (See Ch. VII for
another extract from the speech, explaining the
circumstances which gave rise to the prosecution.)
In the brief period between his return from exile
and the Conference of Luca it was Cicero's political
purpose to destroy the First Triumvirate by draw-
ing Pompey over to the Optimates and to reactivate
the alliance of Senate and equites (concordia ordinum) on which he had relied in 63 and in which he
placed so much hope. Hence, the unusually generous criteria for membership of the Optimates, with
their inherently conservative ideal, cum dignitate
otium, and the moral and social condemnation of
the Populares.

96. There have always been two categories of men in
this state who have desired to take a prominent part in
politics; of these two categories the one has aimed at
being by repute and in reality 'populares', the other
'optimates'. Those who made it their object to do and say
what was agreeable to the people were thought of as
'populares', while the 'optimates' were those who acted in
such a way as to make their policies acceptable to all the
97. best citizens. Who then do I mean by 'best citizens'?
Let me tell you in answer to your question that they are
countless in number, for our country could not otherwise
stand firm. The optimates include those who direct the

policy of the state in the Senate and their supporters; they include the men in the highest orders in the State, who are eligible for the Senate; they include Roman citizens living in the municipia or in the country areas; they include business men, and even freedmen as well. As I have said, this category comprises many and various types of person, but to remove any possible misconception the whole category can be defined quite briefly: all are optimates who are not criminals, not naturally unprincipled, not wild revolutionaries or embarrassed by financial difficulties. We may assume then that this 'tribe', as you have called it in a derogatory way, includes everyone who is honest, sound in mind, and financially secure. Those who are guided by the wishes, interests, and views of these men in political affairs are supporters of the optimates, and are themselves reckoned optimates and are classed among our most important and distinguished citizens, as leaders of the state.

98.   What then is the objective of these helmsmen of the state? Where should they fasten their gaze? In what direction should they steer their course? Towards that most excellent and most desirable goal for all sensible, decent[9], well-to-do men - a state in which the desire for civil harmony[3] is balanced by respect for the political ambitions of our leading men[2]. All those who desire this are reckoned optimates; those who can bring it to pass are considered heroes and saviours of the state. Men should not be so carried away by the status[2] which public office can confer that they ignore the need for harmony in the state[3], but neither should they be so eager to have peace[3] at any cost that they neglect the just claims of men of standing[2].

        Now the essential elements of this situation[2, 3], which the leaders must safeguard and defend even at the risk of their lives, are these: fear of the gods, the auspices, the powers of the magistrates, the prestige[1] of the Senate, the laws, the traditions of our ancestors, criminal and civil jurisdiction, financial credit, our provinces, our allies, the glory of our empire, the army, and the treasury.

99. To be champion and patron of these many great institutions requires a man of great spirit, great ability, and great moral courage. For among our large body of citizens there is a very large number of men who are conscious of their crimes and through fear of punishment seek revolution

and the overthrow of the political system, or who, having a perverted taste for destruction, are satisfied only by civil strife and insurrection, or again who, being in financial distress and bound to crash, think it better to bring everyone else down with them. Whenever men like this have found people to protect their criminal interests and put them into effect, storms arise in the state so that those who have claimed the right to stand at its helm must be watchful and must strive with all their skill and all their care to preserve the essential elements of which I have just spoken, to hold on their course, and to reach that harbour in which a state at peace[3] honours its political leaders[2]

100.   If I were to deny, jurors, that this course is stormy, difficult, and full of dangers and snares, I should be telling a lie, and all the more so because I have not only always known the statement to be true, but have myself experienced these dangers more than other men.

The forces which attack the state are greater than those which defend it. Men who are naturally reckless and desperate are set in motion by a mere nod, and then their own natural disposition hurries them forward against the state without prompting. But respectable men[9] for some reason are slower to act; they neglect the initial stages and are eventually aroused at the last moment only by sheer necessity, and sometimes this hesitation and slowness of movement leads to a situation in which, for all their desire to preserve civil harmony [3] even at the cost of some loss

101. in personal prestige[2], they end up without either. Of those who would like to be thought defenders of the state the unreliable desert and the timid are useless. The only ones who stand firm and endure everything for the state are men of the character of your father, M. Scaurus, who from the time of C. Gracchus to that of Q. Varius resisted all attempts at revolution and was never shaken from his purpose by any violence, threats, or unpopularity. Or like Q. Metellus, your mother's uncle; during his censorship, he censured L. Saturninus, who was then at the height of his power in the popular cause, in the face of a violent and angry crowd refused to admit to the citizen lists an imposter claiming to be a Gracchus, and was the only man who refused to swear to obey a law which he had judged to be illegally proposed; after all this, he preferred to leave

Italy than to abandon his principles. Or again, leaving aside examples from the past - though there are many, as one would imagine from the extent of our power[4] - and without mentioning any who are still alive, men of the quality of the late Q. Catulus, who was neither driven from his course by the threat of danger nor enticed from it by the blandishments of office.

102.   In the name of the Immortal Gods I beg you to imitate these examples, if you seek honour[2], praise and glory; these examples are glorious, they are superhuman, they are immortal; they are proclaimed in men's stories, entrusted to the archives of history and transmitted to posterity. The task involves hard work, I do not deny it; and the perils, I admit, are great; as Atreus so truly says in the play of Accius

'Many are the snares for the honourable'[9];

but

'To lay claim to something which many people envy and seek to gain is sheer folly, unless you are prepared to work hard and employ the greatest care'.

I wish Accius had not also provided a quotation for our worthless citizens to seize on:

'let them hate, provided that they fear'.

for the precepts given to our youth in those other words
103. are splendid. But this optimate system of governing the country was formerly more dangerous when it often happened that the desires of the masses or the interests of the people did not coincide with the national interest. When Lucius Cassius introduced a law about the use of a secret ballot, the people thought that its own freedom was at stake; the leaders of the state disagreed and feared the impetuosity of the masses and the licence which the ballot offered, for the interests of the Optimates were at stake. Tiberius Gracchus proposed a land bill which pleased the people and seemed likely to put the fortunes of the lower classes on a secure basis, but the optimates opposed it vigorously because they saw that it was leading to discord and thought evicting the rich from the estates they had held for so long was no better than robbing the state of its champions. Caius Gracchus introduced a corn law; the plebeians were delighted because they were

being presented with food on a generous scale and without having to work for it, but respectable citizens[9] opposed it because they thought that it invited the plebs to abandon hard work for idleness and because they saw that it was a drain upon the treasury.

104.   In my own lifetime too there have been many issues, which I omit intentionally, which were the subject of dispute as the desires of the people conflicted with the advice of our leading men.   But at the present time there is no longer any reason why the people should disagree with the élite, their leaders.   The people makes no demands, is not eager for revolution, and is delighted with the peace[3] it now enjoys, with the prestige[2] enjoyed by all the optimates, and with the glory of the whole state.   Those who wish to incite the Roman people to sedition and riot can no longer arouse them by offers of largesse, because the plebeians have passed through the stage in which the dangerous course of insurrection and strife seemed appropriate and now embrace peace[3];   this is why these revolutionaries are now reduced to hiring audiences for their public meetings.   Their object is not to make speeches and proposals which their audience want to hear;   no, by bribery and corruption they ensure that the audiences seem
105. at least to want to hear whatever they say.   Surely you do not imagine that the Gracchi or Saturninus or any of those people who were considered populares in time past ever had hired audiences at public meetings?   None of them did, because the official distributions and the prospect of advantage offered by the proposal of some law excited the multitude without any need of bribery.   Accordingly in those days the populares did indeed give offence to thoughtful and respectable people but to judge from the demonstrations of popular approval they had considerable support: they were applauded at the theatre, the voters supported their proposals, and their names, speeches, expression, and gait were objects of popular affection.   Their opponents were thought to be important and distinguished men, but, although they carried great weight in the Senate and had particular influence with the respectable [9], they were not acceptable to the multitude.   Their desires were often thwarted by the popular vote.   If ever any one of them was applauded he would fear that he had made some mistake.   And yet in matters of real importance it was by the influence[1] of such men that this same people was most swayed.

Cicero, de lege agraria, II, 1 - 10.

In 63 a tribune, P. Servilius Rullus, brought
forward a wide-ranging agrarian bill which was
thought to have the backing of Crassus and Caesar
and was directed against Pompey's political interests in anticipation of his return from the East.
Cicero had already attacked the proposal in the
Senate and now used the occasion of his first speech
to the people as consul to attack it again. In the
political circumstances of the year it is easy to
appreciate his insistence on the fact that Catiline
and Rullus (or his backers) are not the only men
with the interests of the people at heart. (For an
earlier example of a speech by a popularis see Ch.I.)

1. It is an old and well-established custom, citizens,
that those whom you have honoured with the consulship,
and whose portrait busts may thus be placed among their
ancestors', should in their first public speech combine an
expression of their gratitude towards you for the favour
you have shown them with praise of their ancestors. On
these occasions it sometimes happens that a man proves
himself worthy of the position attained by his ancestors,
but generally all these men do is to make it seem as if you
have not paid in full the sum you owe their ancestors but
are still in debt to their descendants. I cannot speak to
you about my ancestors, citizens; not because they were
any different from what you see me to be - I am of their
blood and trained according to their principles - but because they took no part in politics and thus never enjoyed
the glory and renown you can confer on a man by electing

2. him to high office. If I were to speak to you about myself,
I am afraid I might seem conceited, while not to do so
might seem ungrateful. For it is very difficult for me to
mention myself the efforts by which I have achieved this
distinction[2] and yet I cannot possibly pass over in silence
the favours you have done me. For this reason I shall
adopt a strictly cautious procedure in my speech and,
while I recall how much I owe you, shall discreetly venture
to explain why I deserve the great esteem in which you
hold me and the high office to which you have elected me,
hoping that your opinion of me will remain what it has
always been.

3.   I am the first new man whom you have made consul for a very long time, the first, one might almost say, within living memory. Under my leadership you have stormed the citadel which the nobility had fortified so carefully and kept under such close guard and have shown that in future you wish its gates to stand wide open to the claims of merit. It is not simply that you have made me consul, in itself a great honour, but that you have done so in a way few nobles in this city have ever become consul and, before me, no new man. Certainly, if you consider what happened to other new men, you will find that those who reached the consulship at their first attempt stood for election many years after they had been praetor, when they were well past the minimum age set by law, and that they all owed their success to continual effort and to a happy choice of the right year to stand; but those who were candidates at the minimum age were never elected on their first attempt. I am the only one of all the new men we can remember who both stood for office at the minimum age and was elected at the first attempt. These facts make it impossible for anyone to claim that the honour which I have received from you was snatched from some other candidate or won only after continual requests; I stood for the consulship at the correct point in my career, and my success must be seen as the

4.   reward of merit[2].   I repeat, citizens; it is indeed a great honour that I am the first new man to become consul for many years, that I was elected in the first year in which I was a candidate, and that I was a candidate at the minimum age permitted by law; but nothing can be more glorious or splendid than the fact that, when you elected me consul, you did so not in silence, relying on the ballot to protect your freedom of choice, but openly, raising your voices as an indication of your goodwill towards me and enthusiasm for my cause.   My election as consul did not remain in doubt until all the votes were counted but was clear from the very moment you began to assemble; it was proclaimed not by the successive announcements of the various heralds but by a single unanimous shout from the entire Roman people.

5.   This favour you have shown me, citizens, is exceptional, indeed unique; I recognize that it brings me considerable gratification and delight but also, and to an even greater extent, worry and concern.   I am continually prey to anxieties of the most serious nature, which allow me no rest either by day or by night.   Above all, I must protect the office of

consul, a task difficult and worrying enough for any man, but particularly so for me. If I make a mistake, I cannot hope for pardon, and, if I succeed, I shall receive but slight and grudging praise. I cannot count upon the faithful advice of the nobility when I am uncertain what to do, nor

6. upon their unquestioning support when I am in danger. But if the risk were mine alone, citizens, I could bear it more easily. I have the impression, though, that there are certain men who will take advantage of any mistake I may make, whether it really deserves censure or is purely accidental, to find general fault with you all for preferring me to the nobility. My object, however, must be to ensure that all my actions and all my decisions are greeted with praise for your action in deciding to elect me consul, and I consider that I should be prepared to suffer any fate rather than fail in this. What makes my task as consul even more difficult and dangerous is that I have decided that I should not follow the same rules or act on the same principles as previous holders of this office. Some of them, indeed, have gone to great lengths to avoid coming here and speaking to you face to face, while the others have done so only reluctantly. As for me, the promise I am about to make you here, where it is an easy thing to say, I have already made in the Senate, where such language seemed quite out of place; as I said there in my first speech, on 1st January, I shall be a people's consul.

7. I realize that I owe my election, in which I far outstripped men of the highest nobility, not to the support of a group of powerful men nor to the far-reaching influence of a small minority but to the will of the entire Roman people. It is inevitable, then, that both now in my year of office and throughout the rest of my life I shall be seen to be on the side of the people. But in attempting to explain the true force and meaning of this phrase 'a people's consul' I stand in great need of your understanding, for a dangerously misleading impression of its meaning is now becoming current, caused by the hypocritical claims of a group of men who attack and frustrate the true interests and well-being of the people while making it the object of their speeches to win a repu-

8. tation as populares. The state for which I assumed responsibility on 1st January was, I know, deeply affected by terror and anxiety. There was no limit to the fears of respectable men[9], nor to the confident expectations of the wicked; every sort of disaster and calamity was

considered possible. It was reported that all kinds of
revolutionary plots against the present form of government
and against the peace[3] you now enjoy were either being
started or had been in progress from the time when I became consul elect. There was no feeling of confidence in
our public life, but its loss was due not to some sudden
crushing disaster but to suspicion, to disorder in the law
courts and to the invalidating of decisions already reached
in them. There was a general feeling that the aim behind
all this was the re-establishment of dictatorial power[5] in
some new form, that these men would not be satisfied with
constitutional authority [4], on however grand a scale, but
were bent on tyranny[6].

9.   Since I could see this clearly - it was no longer a
matter of merely suspecting it, for they made no attempt
at concealment - I said in the Senate that during my year
of office I should be a people's consul. For what is so
dear to the people as peace? Not only those creatures
endowed by nature with feeling, but the very buildings and
fields seem to delight in it. What is so dear to the people
as liberty ? It is a matter of common knowledge that not
men alone but even the beasts of the field long for liberty
and consider it more important than everything else. What
is so dear to the people as harmony within the state[3] ?
You and your ancestors, and indeed all men of spirit, value
it so highly that they are prepared to undertake any labour,
however difficult, which may one day lead to this goal, particularly if it can be combined with a position of authority[4]
and prestige[2]. Moreover it is for this that we are most
indebted to our ancestors; it is their labours that have
made it possible for us to enjoy this harmony[3] without
risk. How then can I fail to support the people, when I
see that all these benefits - peace on our frontiers, the
liberty which is characteristic of your race and reputation,
harmony within the state[3] - in short, all the things you
hold precious, have been entrusted to my faithful care and
that, as consul, I have become in some sense the patron of
10. your interests? Furthermore, citizens, when you hear
the announcement of some largesse, which can easily be
made to sound attractive but cannot possibly be put into
effect without exhausting the treasury, you should not welcome it nor consider it in your interests. As for disturbances in the law courts, the invalidating of decisions
already made, the restoration to condemned men of their

public rights - these are usually the signs of a state already doomed and mark the last stages of its destruction; they cannot possibly be considered in the people's interest.   And if there are men who hold out to the Roman people the hope of land grants but whose secret purpose is quite different from their public claims, they do not deserve the name of populares.

[Q. Cicero], Handbook on Electioneering, 13 - 24.

> The Handbook on Electioneering purports to be a letter to Marcus Cicero from his brother Quintus offering advice on the conduct of his campaign for the consulship. Its authenticity has been much discussed (Henderson, JRS, 40, 1950; Nisbet, JRS, 51, 1961; Balsdon, CQ, 56, 1963), but whatever its authorship and date of composition it provides a valuable picture of electioneering in the late republic. (A translation of the whole letter is published in LACTOR 3)

13.   Since I have explained what assets you possess and could possess to counter-balance your lack of nobility, I think I ought now to speak about the importance of the election campaign. You are a candidate for the consulship, an office which everyone thinks you deserve, but which some begrudge you. For although you are a person of the equestrian order by origin, you are seeking the highest position in the state, highest in the sense that the same office confers much more distinction upon a man of bravery, eloquence, and purity of life than on others. Do not imagine that those who have held that office fail to see what degree of political esteem[2] you too will enjoy once you have obtained it. I suspect indeed that those who, though born of consular families, have not attained the position of their ancestors, are jealous of you, except for any individuals who are particularly fond of you. Even new men who have been praetors, I think, unless obliged to you for some act of kindness on your part, do not like the

14. idea of your reaching higher office than they have. Now I am sure you are aware that many among the people are jealous, that many have become disenchanted with new men because of recent precedents. Several too are bound to be annoyed with you because of the cases you have pleaded. Furthermore, consider carefully whether you suppose any people to be opposed to you because you applied

15. yourself with such enthusiasm to promoting Gnaeus Pompeius' glory. Therefore, since you are seeking the highest office of state and see that there are interests which oppose you, you must consider your position carefully and must apply yourself to the task with the utmost diligence and determination.

16. An election campaign for public office is divisible into two types of activity, one concerned with securing the support of friends, the other, the sympathies of the people. The support of friends must be won by acts of kindness arising spontaneously or from obligation, by length of acquaintance, by charm and amiability of personality. But this term 'friends' has a wider application during an election campaign than at any other time in one's life; for anyone who shows any degree of sympathy towards you, who pays attention to you, who frequents your house, must be included in the category of 'friends'. However, it is particularly advantageous to be popular and well-liked among those who are friends on the more regular grounds of relationship by blood or marriage, membership of the same club, or some

17. close connexion. Next you must take great pains that any who are on intimate terms with you, particularly members of your household, should favour you and desire you to be as successful as possible; then also members of your tribe, neighbours, clients, freedmen too, and last of all even your slaves; for virtually all the talk which develops into the gossip of the forum originates from sources within the home. In fine, friends of every class must be organised; as figureheads, men famous for their office or name (who, even if they do not give practical assistance in canvassing, nevertheless confer some political esteem[2] upon the candidate); for guaranteeing your right to stand, magistrates (particularly the consuls and after them the tribunes of the plebs); for securing the votes of the centuries, men of exceptional influence.[8] Work especially hard to win and retain the support of such men as have or hope to have your influence to thank for the vote of a tribe or century or some other advantage; for in recent years men of ambition have striven with all their zeal and effort to be sure of gaining what° they request from the members of their tribe; you should endeavour in every possible way to ensure that these men are enthusiastic for your cause from the bottom of their hearts and with total devotion.

19.   But if people were as grateful as they should be, all this support should already be available to you, as indeed I trust it is.   During the past two years you have placed four political clubs under obligation to yourself, those of Gaius Fundanius, Quintus Gallius, Gaius Cornelius, and Gaius Orchivius - all men of great influence[8] in electoral matters;   when they committed their cases to your care, these men came under an obligation to you and have promised to fulfil it, as I myself know, for I was present. You must now demand repayment of their debts by frequent reminders, appeals, and assurances;   take care that they understand that they will never have any other opportunity of showing their gratitude.   They will certainly be roused to active support for you through hope of your reciprocal services in the future, as well as by reason of the favours

20. you have recently done them.   In sum, since your candidature is mainly founded upon the sort of friends you have gained by defending them in the courts, see that every one of those under an obligation to you has his individual task clearly defined and specified.   You have never troubled any of them before in any way;   make sure they realize that this is the moment for which you have reserved all the debts you consider they owe you.

21.   Three main factors induce men to display good-will and to support a candidate enthusiastically in his campaign; a favour, future prospects, or like-mindedness and sympathy. Observe, then, how to take care of each of these categories. Quite small favours are considered sufficient grounds for a man to lend his support at the poll, and assuredly those whose acquittal you have secured - and there are many of them - cannot fail to realize that if they do not do enough for you at this crucial time they will never win anybody's approval.   Despite this, they must be asked personally and even led to believe that we think ourselves put under an obligation in turn to those who have hitherto been obliged

22. to us.   As for those who are bound to us by the hope of future prospects, a class of people still more attentive and punctilious about their duties, make sure it is clear to them that your aid is always ready and available, and that they understand that you are carefully watching the services they render;   it will then be obvious that you see and fully

23. appreciate the help you receive from each of them.   The third category of support is spontaneous sympathy.   This

group you will have to secure by expressions of thanks, by suiting your remarks to the motives for which each seems enthusiastic for your cause, by indicating equal good-will towards them, and by encouraging them to hope for a closer degree of friendship. In all these categories you must judge and weigh the potential of each, so that you may know both how far you should pay attention to each and what you can expect and demand of each.

24.   There are certain men, influential[8] in their own districts or municipia, men of energy and affluence, who may not have cultivated this influence[8] previously, but can readily work hard to suit the occasion for the sake of one towards whom they feel obligation or sympathy. You must pay attention to these types of men and make them realise that you see what you can expect of each, appreciate what you receive, and remember what you have received. There are other men, however, who either have no influence or are actually disliked by the members of their tribe and lack the spirit or the ability to exert themselves on the spur of the moment. See that you can distinguish these from the others, and do not put greater reliance on them than the amount of help they actually provide will justify.

Cicero, pro Murena, 21 - 25.

L. Licinius Murena was elected consul for 62 and then immediately prosecuted for bribery (ambitus) by one of his defeated rivals, Servius Sulpicius Rufus. Danger still threatened from the Catilinarians, and Cicero based his defence on the need to have an active and experienced soldier in office at the start of 62.

21.   Each of them is a man of the greatest distinction and the greatest merit[2]; and if Servius allowed me to, I would judge their merits equal and worthy of the same praise. But no! he attacks the military life, lays into the whole of Murena's service as legate, and thinks that the consulship is a matter only of one's constant presence in the Forum and a succession of daily legal tasks. "Do you mean to tell me that you've been with the army", says he, "and haven't been near the Forum for so many years? And when after this prolonged absence you finally appear, are you to compete for position with those who have made

the Forum their home?". To begin with, Servius, this continuous presence of ours: you don't realize how men can sometimes have too much of it, become bored by it. Certainly it stood me in excellent stead that my populari- ty[8] was before the eyes of all; but it was only by great efforts on my own part that I overcame men's boredom with me, and, I dare say, you have done so too; all the same, it would have been no bad thing for either of us if men had felt our absence.

22.   If I may leave this aside, however, and return to the comparison of your respective callings and skills, how can there be any doubt that, when it comes to getting the con- sulship, the glory of a military career produces far grea- ter distinction[2] than the glory which comes from civil law? You get up long before dawn to prepare opinions for your clients; he does so, in order to reach his des- tination with his army in good time. You are woken by the cock's crow, he by the sound of the bugle; you draw up a case, he draws up a line of battle. You guard against your clients being convicted, he against cities or camps being captured; he uses his skill and knowledge to keep off the forces of the enemy, you to keep out rain- water. He is well practised in extending boundaries, you in delimiting them. Small wonder, indeed, - for I must express what I feel - that excellence in the art of war out- shines all other virtues. It is this that has won for the Roman people its name, and for our city imperishable glory; it is this that has compelled the world to acknow- ledge our sway[4]; all our business in the city, all these precious occupations of ours, our fame at the bar, our hard work, lie safe under the protection and defence of martial valour. The moment a hint of war makes itself heard, our skills fall silent at once.

23.   Now as you appear to me to be caressing this legal knowledge of yours as though it were your dear little daughter, I do not propose to let you linger under such a delusion as to think that this thing - whatever it is - that you have so laboriously learned is really anything very special. Because of your other qualities - your self- control, your dignity, your sense of justice, your honesty - I have always considered you fully deserving of the con- sulship, and indeed of every distinction; but as for your mastery of the civil law, I will not call it wasted labour,

but I will say that there is no beaten path to the consulship
in that field of study.   All such professions as serve to
win us the support of the Roman people ought to possess
an intrinsic merit[2] that men can admire and a usefulness
24. that earns great popularity.   The highest merit[2] resides
in those who have won outstanding glory in war;   every -
thing in the empire[4], every element in our constitution,
is, we believe, defended and strengthened by them;   they
are also the most useful, if it is indeed true that by their
advice and by the dangers they undergo, we are enabled
to enjoy not only our political life but also our very property.   Another thing that is important and of great worth[2]
is the power of eloquent speech, a thing which has often
proved decisive in the election of a consul - the power to
sway the hearts of senate, people or jury by reasoned
oratory.   We are looking for a consul who by his oratory
can sometimes check the frenzied agitations of the tribunes,
appease the excitement of the people, and stand out against
bribery.   It is not surprising if men who were often not
even of noble birth have achieved the consulship by this
power of theirs, particularly when at the same time it earns
them the widest popularity[8], the most steady alliances,
and the most solid support.   But none of this is true of that
25. trade of yours, Sulpicius.   First, such a trifling subject
can possess no intrinsic worth[2]: its matter is insignificant, being virtually taken up with individual letters and
word-divisions.   Secondly, even if your calling did possess
something that aroused the admiration of our forefathers,
this has come utterly into contempt now your mystic arts
have been divulged.   Once upon a time, only a few men
knew whether or not legal proceedings could be taken: for
the official calendar was not public property.   Those who
were consulted on legal matters were in a very powerful
position: men would actually ask them for the right day,
as if they were astrologers!   But then a clerk, one Gnaeus
Flavius, was found, a man who could out-smart the smart-
est, and by learning off the individual days he published the
calendar, and filched their knowledge from under the very
noses of these canny lawyers.   This made them angry, and
they were afraid that now the list of days was published and
understood men could go to law without their help: they
therefore concocted some legal formulae to enable them to
have a finger in every pie.

V

THE CATILINARIAN CONSPIRACY

The survival of Cicero's speeches against Catiline and of Sallust's monograph about the conspiracy make this a prominent incident in the history of the late republic.

Catiline had served as a legate under Sulla in the Civil War and proscriptions.   In 68 he became praetor and after a term of office as governor of Africa returned to Rome in 66 with the intention of standing for the consulship of 65.   An impending prosecution for extortion led to his being barred from the elections, and this in coincidence with other disturbances gave rise to rumours of a coup d'état – the so-called First Conspiracy of Catiline.   (For an examination of the unsubstantial nature of the evidence for this plot see H. Frisch, Classica et Mediaevalia, IX, 1947 and R. Seager, Historia, 13, 1964.)   In 65 Catiline's trial again prevented his standing in the consular elections, and in 64, when his candidacy was accepted, he was pushed into third place in the poll by an electoral pact between Cicero and C. Antonius.

The conspiracy of Catiline was not the only problem with which Cicero had to contend as consul. The year 63 was overshadowed by the imminent return of Pompey from the East and was marked in its earlier months by various political moves on the part of Caesar and his political associates – the agrarian bill of Rullus (see Ch. III), Caesar's election as Pontifex Maximus, and his prosecution of Rabirius – and towards its close by the prosecution of Murena (see Ch. IV) and the attacks on Cicero of the tribune Metellus Nepos.

At the consular elections for 62 Catiline was again defeated and then adopted a more violent course. His conspiracy involved a series of armed risings in various parts of Italy, in particular Etruria, and simultaneously a terrorist campaign of murder and arson in Rome.   On 21st October Cicero was able to reveal Catiline's plans to the Senate and the Senatus Consultum Ultimum was passed.   On 8th November, after Cicero had attacked him directly in the Senate (the First Speech against Catiline), Catiline left Rome. In the Second Speech, delivered on the next day, Cicero explained the situation to the people. Although Catiline had left Rome, the other conspirators remained at large in the city as Cicero had insufficient evidence to arrest them. At the end of November they approached a deputation of the Allobroges (a Gallic tribe) then visiting Rome and tried to enlist their support for the plot. The Allobroges' patron in Rome, Q. Fabius Sanga, passed the information to Cicero, and on 3rd December the conspirators were arrested. On the same day Cicero again spoke to the people (Third Speech). On 5th December in the senatorial debate upon the punishment appropriate for the conspirators, Cicero delivered the Fourth Speech supporting the proposal made by the consul-elect Decimus Silanus that they should be put to death. This view was contested by Caesar but carried after an impressive speech in its favour by Cato. (See Sallust, Catiline, 50.4 - 53.1) The conspirators were executed that night. Early in 62 Catiline's forces were defeated and he himself was killed in a hard fought battle near Pistoria.

CATILINE'S CHARACTER

Sallust, Catilinae Coniuratio, 5.

5. Lucius Catilina belonged to a noble family. He had great mental and physical energy, but his abilities were perverted and destructive. From his boyhood he had revelled in civil war, murder, robbery, and public discord, and it was in such activities that he had employed his youth. His physical strength enabled him to bear hunger, cold, and lack of sleep to an incredible degree; he was daring, cunning, and adaptable, quite capable of pretending support for any policy and of concealing his true opinion; greedy for other people's money, extravagant with his own, and passionately enthusiastic in pursuit of all his aims. He was a reasonably fluent speaker, but lacked discretion. His boundless ambition was constantly directed towards wildly fantastic and unattainable ends. After the dictatorship[5] of Sulla he was possessed by a tremendous urge to seize control of the government and he did not in the least mind what methods he used, provided he obtained supreme power[6].

Poverty and a guilty conscience, both of which had been increased by the activities described above, each day further provoked his uncontrolled ambition. He was also encouraged by the corrupt state of public morality, which was being undermined by two equally terrible but very different evils - avarice and extravagance.

Since I have had occasion to speak of public morality, the nature of my material seems to suggest that I should go further back and give a brief account of the domestic and foreign policy of our ancestors; how they governed the country, how powerful it was when they left it to us, and how it has gradually changed from its former excellence and distinction and has now plumbed the depths of wickedness and disgrace.

Cicero, pro Caelio, 12 - 14.

In 56 Cicero defended M. Caelius Rufus upon a charge of violence (vis). Although Caelius' association with Catiline was not strictly relevant to the charge it had clearly done his reputation no good, and Cicero has to handle the point with some care.

12.   Yes, I grant you that Caelius supported Catiline politically when he had already spent several years in public life. Many others of every class and age did the same, for Catiline had in him, as you may remember, many marks of excellence not firmly developed but apparent in outline.

He might frequent many men of the worst character, but equally he at least pretended to be dedicated to those of the best. Men found in him not only many enticements to vice but also definite incentives to hard work: he was a firebrand of profligacy, yet had as keen an appetite for military life. I believe there has never been such an extraordinary being on earth, endowed with such opposite,
13. divergent, and incompatible passions and appetites. At one time, no-one was more attractive to men of repute yet more hand in glove with villains. You could not have found a more loyal citizen at one stage, yet who was a more foul traitor to his country? Who has been more debauched or more grasping, yet who more industrious or more generous? There were, then, gentlemen, these extraordinary contradictory qualities in him: his ability to win many friends and to keep them by devoted service;

to share all he had with everybody; to meet the critical needs of his followers with money, influence[8], physical effort, even crime, if need be, of the most outrageous nature; to adapt, discipline, and manipulate himself to meet every occasion. Thus was he able to behave with austerity among the puritanical, with gaiety among the lax, to be serious with the older generation, affable with the young, a daredevil to those of criminal inclinations, and a

14. roué among the debauched. With this adaptable and complex make-up, he not only won over to him all the boldest scoundrels in the world but also began to influence many honest men with this facade of virtue. For Catiline could never have initiated his criminal and treasonable onslaught on our empire[4], had there not been basic qualities of adaptability and endurance beneath the appalling vice. So, gentlemen, you must reject this charge against Caelius of alleged intimacy with Catiline, for many honest men have shared this failing. Even I myself was once almost deceived by him, when I thought him honourable and of honourable designs, a true and loyal friend. I never suspected his crimes till forced to by the evidence of my own eyes; indeed I had no idea of their existence, until I held the evidence in my own hands. If the young Caelius was one of this throng which gathered around Catiline, he ought to be vexed at having made a mistake - just as I frequently repent my mistaken trust in him - but not have to stand in fear of the charge of being "a friend of Catiline".

CATILINE'S SUPPORTERS

Cicero, in Catilinam, II, 17-23.

17. I will firstly, citizens, reveal to you the different groups that make up Catiline's forces: then I shall give you, for each particular group, whatever intelligent remedy my speech can suggest.

18. The first group are those who are steeped in debt yet refuse to solve the problem by relinquishing the ample properties they love so much. Outwardly these men seem honourable - for they are wealthy - but their intentions and policy are shameless. You, sir, apparently wealthy and cosseted, with your lands and houses, your silver and property, why do you hesitate to surrender just a little of this to win back your credit? Are you hoping for war? Do

you really think that in the universal destruction your property will be sacrosanct? Perhaps you await a list
announcing a general cancellation of debts? Those who
expect this from Catiline are fools. I myself will publish
lists, but they will be lists of property up for auction;
for those who have property cannot become solvent except
by selling it. If only they had been prepared to do this
earlier and had not stupidly decided to try to match the
interest on their loans with the income from their estates,
we would find them now richer and better citizens. But
these fellows, I fancy, are not greatly to be feared because one can either deflect them from their point of view
or, if they persist, they seem more likely to assail the
state with prayers than with arms.

19.   A second group are also debtors, but are men who
expect to rule[5], who wish to seize power, who think that
they can obtain positions in civil war that are closed to
them in peace. These fellows must learn - as indeed all
the others too - to abandon all hope of achieving this: for
in the first place, I am awake and at hand, watching over
the state: secondly, the decent elements[9] in the state
are full of determination, there is a unanimity of feeling
among all classes, and we possess numerical superiority
in the city and in the armed forces: finally, they must
reflect that the gods will, in person, help this invincible
people, this famous empire[4], and this beautiful city to
resist these vast criminal forces. Again, suppose these
criminal lunatics get what they so lust for, do they really
expect, amid the ashes of their city and the blood of their
citizens, to rule as consuls or dictators or kings[6] ?
Don't they see that if they got what they wanted the same
right would have to be given to runaway slaves and gladiators?

20.   There is a third group, now elderly, but tough
through years of training: the scoundrel Manlius, from
whom Catiline is now taking over, is one of these. These
are people from the colonies Sulla set up; taken as a whole,
they are all, I am sure, full of the best and bravest men,
but these particular settlers are men who have, in their
sudden and unlooked-for prosperity, flaunted themselves
too extravagantly and arrogantly. While they build like
millionaires and amuse themselves with choice estates,
large retinues, elaborate banquets, they have fallen into

such debt that they are never likely to become solvent
again - except by recalling Sulla from the dead. They have,
moreover, tainted some of the peasants, men of little
wealth or prospects, with the same hope of plunder. Both
of these groups I class as freebooters and scavengers; I
advise them to pull themselves together and to forget about
proscriptions and dictatorships: for so deeply is the grief
and pain of those days engraved on the heart of the state
that I fancy not even the beasts of the field, never mind the
people, would allow them to return.

21. The fourth group are indeed a motley and seditious
crew, men long since overwhelmed by life, who never
break through to the surface, men who stagger under old
debts, partly through innate idleness, partly by bad manage-
ment, partly by extravagance, men harassed by having to
pay bail, by the trial procedure, by the confiscation of their
property - thousands in all who are said to have left city
and country to flock to Catiline's standard. These people,
I fancy, are not so much eager soldiers as bad debtors. If
these men cannot be solvent, let them collapse instantly,
but in such a way that neither the state nor even their near-
est neighbour may realise it. I do not understand why, if
they cannot live honourably, they should want to die in disgrace or why they should believe they will die less painfully
in a group than alone.

22. A fifth group is made up of murderers and cut-throats
and criminals of all sorts. These I have no interest in
recalling from Catiline. They cannot be torn from him;
so let them die like the brigands they are, since our prison
is not big enough to hold them.

 Finally, there are those who are not only last in place
but last in the way they live; they are closest to Catiline,
his own choice, his bosom friends; you can recognise
them by their combed and gleaming locks, either beardless
or luxuriantly bearded, wearing sleeved tunics reaching to
their ankles, more like veils than togas. They devote their
whole lives and all their waking hours to the vast labour of
23. banqueting all night long. In this herd is found the gambler,
the adulterer, and all the filth of Rome. These charming
and refined lads have learned not only to make love and to
suffer it, to dance and sing, but also to murder with dagger
or poison. You may be sure that, unless these join Catiline

and die, - and even if he himself dies, - they will be a
breeding ground for future Catilines. What do these
wretches want for themselves? They are surely not
going to take their lady friends with them to camp? Yet
how could they survive without them, now the nights have
turned so cold? How will these hardy soldiers endure the
frosts and snows of the Appennines? Unless, of course,
they believe they will bear the winter more easily because
bare is the way they have learnt to dance at their parties!

Sallust, Catilinae Coniuratio, 36.4 - 39.4.

36.4   It was at this time, I think, that the empire of the
Roman people was in its most pitiable state. From east
to west our armies ruled the world; at home there was
peace[3] and prosperity, two things men value above all
else. Yet there were some citizens who were obstinately
determined to ruin themselves and the state. Despite two
senatorial decrees and the offer of a reward, not one person from the huge number who followed Catiline was induced to reveal the plot and not one deserted from Catiline's
camp. It was like a virulent disease which had spread so
widely that the opinions of a majority of our citizens were
infected.

37.   It was not only the conspirators who were infatuated
in this way; the entire plebs was eager for revolution and
supported Catiline's designs, following in this its usual
habit. In every state the poor always envy the respectable[9] and praise the unprincipled, hate what is established
and long for change. Loathing their own situation they are
eager for revolution; turmoil and rioting increase their
strength and cause them no anxiety, for the poor have
nothing to lose.

The urban plebs was particularly violent. There
were many reasons for this. To begin with, the dregs of
society - men conspicuous for the immorality and shame-
lessness of their lives, bankrupts who had squandered the
money they had inherited in loose living, others who had
had to leave home as the result of some scandalous or
criminal act - all these had flowed into Rome as into a
sewer. Then there were many who remembered the
victory of Sulla; they saw that some of his common
soldiers had now become senators and others were so rich

that they could afford to live as extravagantly as kings and
hoped that, if they joined Catiline's army, victory would
bring them similar rewards. Again, young men from the
country areas, who had previously supported themselves
in poverty by working as hired labourers, were attracted
by the doles available in Rome from private individuals and
from the state and had come to prefer a life of idleness[3]
in the city to this thankless toil. These and others like
them were feeding on the misfortunes of the state. It is not
surprising that men of evil character, living in poverty, were
carried away by extravagant hopes and thought little of the
consequences to themselves or to the state. Their view of
the rewards to be won by civil war was shared by the children of the men proscribed by Sulla, whose property had
been confiscated and whose political rights had been restric-
ted. In addition, those who opposed the senatorial party
preferred to see the state in chaos than to find their own
power diminished. This was the evil that had now returned
to plague the state after an absence of many years.

38.   After the restoration of tribunician power in the consulship of Cnaeus Pompeius and Marcus Crassus young men,
whose age intensified their natural aggressiveness, attained
this high office. They begain to stir up the plebs by accu-
sing the Senate, to inflame them still further by doles and
promises, and so to increase their own popularity and power.
The majority of the nobility opposed them with all its might,
ostensibly in support of the Senate's power, but in fact to
defend their own. To put the true position in a few words,
from this time on all those who took a violent line in politics
did so under honourable pretexts, some maintaining that
they were defending the rights of the people, others that their
object was to increase the influence[1] of the Senate, all
claiming that they were acting in the best interests of the
state but in fact contending for personal power. This political struggle was marked by extreme ruthlessness, and
both parties were cruel in victory.

39.   When Pompey was sent to command in the wars against
the pirates and Mithridates, the power of the plebs was
lessened and that of the few increased. The latter controlled
all magistracies, provinces, and other positions of power.
Powerful, secure, and without fear themselves, they made
use of the courts to terrify their opponents, hoping that any
who reached the tribunate would thus be deterred from

violent agitation in their year of office. But once an un-
settled situation offered a chance of revolution, their
opponents took heart again and their enthusiasm for the
old struggle revived.

If Catiline had won the first battle, or even if the
engagement had been indecisive, a great disaster would
certainly have overwhelmed the state. The victors would
not have been permitted to maintain their position for long;
some opponent of greater power would soon have beaten
them into submission and have wrested from their grasp
both power[4] and liberty.

THE TAKING OF THE CONSPIRATORS

Sallust, Catilinae Coniuratio, 44-48

44.   The Allobroges met the other conspirators through
Gabinius, as Cicero had directed. They demanded from
Lentulus, Cethegus, Statilius, and Cassius a written form
of oath, which they could take to their countrymen under
seal; otherwise, they said, it would be very difficult to
persuade them to join such a dangerous undertaking. The
others consented without suspicion and Cassius promised
that he would himself visit Gaul soon; in fact, he left
Rome shortly before the envoys. Lentulus sent Titus
Volturcius of Crotona with the Allobroges so that they
could break their homeward journey and confirm their
alliance with Catiline by giving and receiving pledges.
In addition he personally gave Volturcius a letter for Catiline, the text of which was as follows:

"The bearer will tell you who I am. Remember the
dangers of your position. Act like a man. Consider what
your interests demand and seek help from everyone, even
the lowest."

He added the following verbal message: "What is the
point of refusing to enlist slaves now that you have been declared a public enemy by the Senate? All your orders have
45. been fulfilled in Rome. Do not hesitate to come nearer to
the city." After these arrangements had been completed,
on the night which had been fixed for their departure the
envoys gave a full report to Cicero, and he ordered the
praetors Lucius Valerius Flaccus and Caius Pomptinus to

lay an ambush for the Allobroges and their retinue on the
Mulvian bridge and to arrest them. He took the praetors
completely into his confidence, explaining the reason for
the order and giving them permission to act as circumstances required. As they were trained soldiers they
obeyed orders, quietly posted guards, and occupied the
bridge unobserved. When the envoys and Volturcius
reached the place, they heard the shouts raised on both
sides. The Gauls quickly understood the situation and
immediately surrendered to the praetors; Volturcius at
first defended himself against heavy odds with his sword
and shouted encouragement to the others, but when he
saw that he had been deserted by the envoys he desperately
appealed to Pomptinus, with whom he was acquainted, to
save him. Finally his resistance and confidence collapsed,
and he surrendered to the praetors as if to enemies from
another country.

46.   Full details of this successful action were quickly
sent to the consul by messengers. He was of course delighted but was also rendered extremely anxious. Glad though
he was to learn that the conspiracy had been uncovered and
the country rescued from danger, he was nevertheless
filled with worry and hesitation: important citizens had
been arrested for plotting the vilest treason, and he had to
decide what action to take. He realized that a decision to
punish them would be a heavy responsibility for him to
carry, while failure to do so might well destroy the state.
Steeling his resolve, he ordered Lentulus, Cethegus,
Statilius, and Gabinius to be sent for, together with
Caeparius of Terracina who was getting ready to leave the
city to rouse the slaves in Apulia to revolt. They all
came at once, except Caeparius who had left home shortly
before and fled from Rome once the plot was discovered.
Cicero personally escorted Lentulus, whose rank as
praetor demanded it, into the temple of Concord; the
others, on his orders, were brought in under guard.
There he summoned the Senate, and in a packed house
introduced Volturcius and the envoys. The praetor
Flaccus, as instructed, brought with him the dispatch box
containing the letters he had captured from the envoys.

47. Volturcius was first questioned about his journey and the
letters, then about his plans and intentions. At first he
prevaricated and denied all knowledge of the conspiracy.
Then he was emboldened to speak by the promise of a free

pardon and gave a complete account of what had happened. He stated that he had been admitted to the conspiracy only a few days before by Gabinius and Caeparius and that he knew no more than the envoys, though he had often heard Gabinius say that Publius Autronius, Servius Sulla, Lucius Vargunteius, and many others were in the plot. The Allobroges made the same admissions, and proved Lentulus guilty when he denied it by referring both to the letters and to his favourite topics of conversation. "It is prophesied in the Sibylline books", he would say, "that three Cornelii will rule[6] Rome. Cinna and Sulla were the first two; I am the third who is destined to govern the city." In addition he had been heard to say that this was the twentieth year since the Capitol had been burnt and diviners interpreting portents had frequently foretold that it would be stained with the blood of civil war. Each of the accused acknowledged his own seal, and the letters were read. The Senate then voted that Lentulus should resign from his praetorship and that he and the others should be kept under house arrest. Consequently Lentulus was given into the charge of Publius Lentulus Spinther, who at that time was an aedile; Quintus Cornificius was responsible for Cethegus, Caius Caesar for Statilius, Marcus Crassus for Gabinius, and Cnaeus Terentius, a plain senator, for Caeparius who had just been caught on the run.

48.   Meanwhile the disclosure of the conspiracy led to a complete reversal of opinion among the plebeians. In their desire for political change they had previously been greatly attracted by the possibilities of war, but now they cursed Catiline's plot and lauded Cicero to the skies, showing as much joy and excitement as if they had been rescued from slavery[7]; for of course the burning of Rome, from their point of view, would have been an appalling and immeasurable disaster since they owned only their clothing and other articles in daily use; whereas other acts of war, far from causing them loss, provided them with plunder.

THE FINAL DEBATE

Cicero, in Catilinam, IV, 7 - 10 & 20 - 22.

7.   I see that two proposals have been made so far, the first by Decimus Silanus, whose opinion is that the men who have tried to destroy this state should be put to death, the

45

other by Caius Caesar, who rejects the death penalty but is eager to see all other punishments inflicted in their full rigour. As you can imagine from their rank[2] and from the gravity of the situation, each of them is determined on severe measures. Silanus considers that the men who have plotted against the lives not merely of all of us here in the Senate but also of the Roman people as a whole, who have tried to destroy our empire[4] and blot out the name of Rome, should no longer be permitted to share the air we all breathe and should be executed immediately; he reminds us that we have often employed the death penalty against vicious citizens. Caesar is of the opinion that the gods did not establish death as a punishment but as an inevitable end to our natural life or as a respite from hardship and sorrow. He is supported by the fact that wise men have never been unwilling to face death, while brave men have often advanced to meet it. But imprisonment, and especially life imprisonment, was clearly established as the special punishment for crimes of exceptional wickedness. He proposes that the guilty men should be distributed among the municipia and kept there in prison. But, if we insist on this measure, the citizens of these towns may think we are acting unjustly, while merely to request it might bring other problems. Nevertheless, Senators, if you approve of this proposal, let it be passed.

8. I shall not shirk the ensuing responsibility and shall hope to find some men among the municipia who would consider it beneath their dignity[2] to refuse a request you have made in the interest of our general security. Caesar also proposes a heavy penalty for the municipia if any prisoner escapes. The criminals are to be kept under severe restrictions, in keeping with the terrifying atrocity of their acts. He proposes a binding decree to make it impossible for anyone to reduce their punishment by action either in the Senate or before the People and thus robs them even of hope, traditionally man's sole comfort in adversity. Moreover he proposes that their possessions be confiscated. Life itself is all he leaves the criminals. Had he taken this too, a single moment of pain would have spared them all the manifold agony of body and soul that is the penalty of their crimes. And so it was to find some means of terrifying criminals here on earth that men of earlier times would have had us believe that similar punishments awaited the guilty after death, for they realized that without some such belief there was no reason to be afraid of death.

9.   Now I see what is in my own interest, Senators, If
you adopt the proposal of Caius Caesar, who follows what
we agree to call the 'popular' line in politics, I may in
future have less reason to fear attacks by the populares,
for people will recognize that it was Caesar who thought
up the proposal and put it forward.   But, if you adopt
Silanus' proposal, I may well be letting myself in for
further trouble.   Nevertheless, I shall not set consideration for my personal safety above the good of the state.
We have in Caesar's proposal a pledge of his lasting goodwill
towards the state, as indeed his personal standing[2] and
the distinction of his ancestors led one to expect.   Now
we can see the great difference between the demagogue,
quite without any deeply held convictions, and the man who
can justly be called 'popular'   because he genuinely seeks

10. the people's welfare.   I see that several of those who
would like to be considered populares are not present in
the Senate today;   presumably they wish to avoid having
to vote on a charge involving the lives of Roman citizens.
Yet only the day before yesterday these very men backed
the decree to put Roman citizens in custody and the thanksgiving to myself, while yesterday they supported the move
to reward the witnesses generously.   They have voted for
the arrest of the criminals, for a thanksgiving to the in-
vestigator, and for a reward for the witnesses; their
general opinion about this case must now be clear to
everyone.   It is not that Caius Caesar does not know of
the Sempronian law which protects Roman citizens;   he
realizes, though, that the man who is a public enemy of
the state cannot possibly be a citizen and knows that
Caius Gracchus himself, the author of this law, paid the
penalty of death to the state, a decision later ratified by
the people.   Nor does Caesar think that Publius Lentulus -
for all his extravagant spending - can still be called a
friend of the people,   now that he has plotted the ruin of
the Roman people and the destruction of the city with such
utter lack of pity or restraint.   So even Caesar - for all
his gentleness and humanity - has no scruples about
committing Lentulus to the darkness of life imprisonment
and proposes a decree binding for all time to prevent anyone ever being able to claim credit for reducing his punishment and so prove his adherence to the popular cause
to the ruin of the Roman people.   He also proposes the
confiscation of their property, so that on top of all their
mental and physical anguish they may not even escape
poverty and beggary.

----

20.   Now before I ask you to vote, I shall make a few brief remarks about my own position. You see how numerous the conspirators are. I am well aware that I have incurred the enmity of each and every one of them, but I consider them base, weak and insignificant. Yet if ever a time comes when some wicked and depraved man can rouse them and they come to have more power than a general recognition of your prestige[2] and of the state's would allow; even then, Senators, I shall never feel that I have acted wrongly myself or encouraged you to do so. They may threaten to kill me, but death awaits all men. But no-one else has ever won such glory in his lifetime as your decrees have bestowed on me; decrees of public thanksgiving to other men have always been a reward for their service to the state, but I am the only man to be so honour-

21. ed for preserving our country from destruction. No-one can deny the glory of Scipio, whose determined strategy forced Hannibal to leave Italy and return to Africa. There can be no question as to the exceptional merit of the second Africanus, who destroyed Carthage and Numantia, two cities which dangerously threatened this empire[4]. We admit the outstanding success of Lucius Aemilius Paulus, whose triumph was adorned by the presence of Perses, once a mighty and famous monarch. Marius twice saved Italy from blockade and freed us from the threat of slavery[7], and his distinction will never be forgotten. Pompey, who swept in glorious success through all lands under the sun, outshines them all. All these are justly praised, but I feel confident that my own achievement will rank among them – unless, of course, you consider it a greater distinction to extend our empire by opening up new provinces than to ensure that our victorious generals and soldiers may have

22. some home to which they can return. And yet in one respect success in a war overseas is better than victory in a civil war. Foreign enemies are either crushed and become slaves or are accepted as friends and consider themselves bound by ties of gratitude. With citizens the position is more difficult; a kind of criminal madness possesses them, and, once they have started to work openly against their own country, you may prevent them destroying the state but you will never be able to crush them by force or win them over by kindness. I realize, therefore, that my war against these criminals will never end. But I rely both upon your support and that of all respectable

citizens[9] and upon the fact that the terrible dangers
from which the Roman people have been saved will not
be forgotten either here in Rome or anywhere else in
the world and am confident that I and my supporters will
not come to any harm at their hands. For it is quite
certain that no force will ever be found strong enough
to shatter your alliance with the equites or to destroy
the current powerful unanimity of opinion among all
decent citizens[9].

VI

THE FIRST TRIUMVIRATE

The First Triumvirate was an unofficial political alliance between Caesar, Pompey, and Crassus,
and despite Suetonius' statement below it may well
have originated before the consular elections in 60.
The specific objectives of each were: for Caesar,
the consulship, followed by a major provincial command; for Pompey, ratification of his Eastern
settlement and a grant of land for his veterans; for
Crassus, a renegotiation of the bad bargain made by a
company of tax-gatherers (publicani) in contracting
for the tithes of the province of Asia. It seems that
the Triumvirs would have been glad of Cicero's support, or even of his silence, but, when it became clear
that he was opposed to them, P. Clodius, who had
been elected tribune for 58, was allowed to press home
his attack upon Cicero for having executed the Catili-
narian conspirators without trial. In 58 Cicero was
driven into exile, to be recalled a year later. (See
Ch. VII).

In January 59 Caesar proposed an agrarian law,
assigning public land in Italy for distribution to Pompey's veterans and the urban plebs and authorizing the
purchase of further land from the revenues of Pompey's
conquests. The proposal was bitterly opposed by
Bibulus, who tried to veto its passage through the
Comitia Tributa on the grounds that the omens were
unfavourable (obnuntiatio) but was prevented from so
doing by organized violence. He then retired to his
house and remained there for the rest of the year,
attempting to vitiate subsequent Caesarian measures
by further use of obnuntiatio. It seems probable,
though, that an announcement of unfavourable omens
had to be made in person on the spot and that Bibulus'
obstruction may itself have thus been technically in-
valid. (See A.W. Lintott, Violence in Republican
Rome, 144 ff. For another example of obnuntiatio,
where the physical presence of the obstructor is important, see Ch. VII, Cicero, ad Att, IV, iii.) A
further agrarian law, dealing with the ager Campanus,
was passed in May; it is this that is referred to in

<u>ad Att,</u> II, xviii, 2 and xix, 4.

Cicero's view that the Triumvirate had destroyed the republic was also held by later writers. C.
Asinius Pollio (cos 40 BC) began his history of the
Civil Wars with the year 60, and Plutarch twice
quotes Cato as claiming that the alliance of Pompey
and Caesar had done the state more harm than their
subsequent quarrel. (Plutarch, <u>Caesar</u>, 13; <u>Pom-
pey</u>, 47.) (See also Syme, <u>Roman Revolution</u>,
Intro.)

Suetonius, <u>Divus Julius</u>, 10; 19; 20.2.

10.   As aedile Caesar embellished not only the comitium,
the forum, and the basilicas but also the Capitol with tem-
porary colonnades, erected to display part of the huge mass
of equipment for use in his shows. He also exhibited wild
beast hunts and games, both with his colleague Bibulus and
on his own; but in either case Caesar alone took the credit
for the money they had spent together. His colleague Marcus Bibulus did not hide his feelings on the matter: 'The
same thing has happened to me,' he used to say, 'as happened to Pollux; for just as the temple in the forum was
dedicated to both the brothers but is simply called Castor's,
so our combined generosity is credited to Caesar alone.'
In addition Caesar also held a gladiatorial display, though
with somewhat fewer pairs than he had planned. For,
when his opponents became frightened by the huge troops
which had been assembled from all parts, a law was passed
limiting the number of gladiators which any one man might
have in Rome.

19.   Of his two competitors for the consulship, Lucius
Lucceius and Marcus Bibulus, Caesar joined forces with
Lucceius, making the bargain that the latter, who had more
wealth but less influence[8], should promise the electorate
money from his own pocket in their joint names. When
this became known, the optimates, afraid that, once he became consul, Caesar would stick at nothing if he had a colleague who supported him wholeheartedly, authorised
Bibulus to promise an equal sum. Many of them contributed money, and even Cato did not deny that this act of
bribery was for the good of the state.

In this way Caesar was elected consul with Bibulus as his colleague. And with the same motives, the optimates took great care that provinces of minimal importance should be assigned to the consuls-elect - the supervision of woods and pastures, in fact. Furious at this insult, Caesar sought the support of Pompey, who was annoyed with the Senate because they were making difficulties over the ratification of the decisions he had made after his victory over Mithridates. Caesar also reconciled Pompey and Marcus Crassus, though they had been inveterate enemies since the days of their joint consulship, which had been marked by total lack of accord. He entered into a pact with them both that nothing should be done in the state to which any of the three objected.

20.2.   From the time Bibulus retired to his house, Caesar ran the state on his own and as he fancied. So much so, indeed, that several wits used to pretend to be witnessing legal documents and jokingly wrote 'witnessed in the consulship of Julius and Caesar' rather than 'in the consulship of Caesar and Bibulus', thus mentioning the same man twice, by his nomen and cognomen. As a result, such lines as the following soon became popular among the people:

> 'It was done in the consulship of Caesar, not Bibulus; for in Bibulus' consulship nothing, as I recall, was done.'

Cicero, ad Atticum, II, xviii, 1 & 2

Rome;   June 59.

1.   I have received several letters from you and now realize how keenly, not to say anxiously, you long to learn what news there is. We are hemmed in on all sides and no longer make any objection to our slavery[7], but dread death and banishment, really the lesser evils, as if they were the greater. Everybody complains about the situation, but no-one says anything to improve it. Those in power, I suspect, intend to leave no-one the opportunity to buy favours. The only man who speaks out openly in opposition is Curio's son. He wins great applause, is warmly greeted in the forum, and moreover gains many signs of favour from respectable citizens[9], who pursue Fufius with shouts, curses, and hisses. But this gives rise, not so much to hope, but rather to indignation when one sees that the people's goodwill

2. is unrestrained but its power of action shackled. But to
    save you asking about everything in detail, the whole affair
    has come to such a pass that there is no hope that the
    magistrates, let alone individual citizens, will ever be
    free. Yet, in the midst of this oppression, our conversa-
    tion, at least at social gatherings and over the dinner-table,
    is freer than it was. Disgust begins to conquer fear,
    without, however, preventing a general despondency about
    everything. The Lex Campana contains a curse to be in-
    voked on themselves by candidates for office if they make
    any proposal that the land should be held under other terms
    than those of the Julian laws. The rest have not hesitated
    to swear to this, but Laterensis, who withdrew his candi-
    dacy for the tribunate so as not to have to take the oath, is
    thought to have acted splendidly.

Cicero, ad Atticum, II, xix.

Rome, July 59.

1.   I have many anxieties arising from the grave political
    situation and from the dangers which threaten me personally.
    They are countless but none is more annoying to me than the
    manumission of Statius:

> 'That my authority[4], no, I let that pass, that my
> displeasure be not even heeded.'

I do not know what to do and it is not so much what has
happened as what is being said. However I cannot even be
angry with those I love dearly. I am simply hurt - and
deeply hurt at that. My other anxieties concern important
matters. The threats of Clodius and the campaigns prepared against me disturb me little: for I think I can face
them all with dignity[1] or avoid them without personal
inconvenience. Perhaps you will say "Enough of dignity.[1]
That's out of date. Please, I beg you, take thought for
your security." Oh dear! why are you not here? I'm
sure nothing would escape your notice. Perhaps I'm
2. blind and too attached to the ideal. You may be certain
    that nothing has ever been so infamous, so disgraceful, so
    generally odious to men of all sorts, classes, and ages as
    the present state of affairs; more so, in truth, than I
    would have wished, let alone imagined. Those "populares"
    have taught even moderate men to hiss. Bibulus is praised
    to the skies - why I don't know - just as though:

> 'One man alone, by delay, restored the state for us.'

Pompeius, my hero, has brought about his own ruin, a fact which causes me great pain. They hold no one by goodwill. I fear they may have to resort to terror. But I do not oppose their cause because of my friendship with him. I do not approve it either. That would be to nullify all I have
3. done previously. I keep to the highway. The feeling of the people has been manifested particularly at the theatre and the shows. For at the gladiatorial show, the master and his guests were overwhelmed with hisses. At the Games of Apollo, the tragic actor Diphilus made a vicious attack on our Pompeius:

> 'To our sorrow you are great .....'

It received a thousand encores. He spoke the line

> 'A time will come when you will rue that same prowess.'

to shouts from the whole theatre. Other lines received the same response. For the lines are such that you might think that they had been written for the occasion by an enemy of Pompeius.

> 'If neither laws nor customs compel.......'

and other lines were spoken amid loud groans and shouts. When Caesar entered, the applause died. Curio's son followed him. He was applauded just as Pompeius used to be when the republic was in good health. Caesar was annoyed, and people say a letter is on its way post-haste to Pompeius at Capua. They are hated by the Equites, who stood and applauded Curio. They are public enemies of all. They threaten the Roscian law and even the corn law. Things really are in a pretty mess. For my part, I should have preferred their undertaking to be passed over in silence, but I fear this may not be possible. People are not tolerating what apparently they must. All now speak with one voice, but this unanimity is based only on hatred, not on strength.

4.   Our friend Publius is constantly threatening me; he is hostile. The business is looming up and you will, I'm sure, come in haste for it. I think I have the sure support of the army of loyalists[9] – the moderately loyal too – the support that I had when I was consul. Pompeius shows considerable favour towards me; he declares that Clodius will not say one word against me. In this he does not

deceive me; he deceives himself. On the death of Cosconius, I was invited to fill his place on the Land Commission for Campania. That would be stepping into a dead
man's shoes! Nothing would have degraded me more in
men's eyes, nothing could have been further removed from
that security you are always talking about. For the Com-
missioners are unpopular with the decent citizens[9], I with
the law-breakers; I should have kept my own unpopularity

5. and taken on other people's as well. Caesar wants me to
join his staff - a more honourable way out of the danger,
certainly, but that's not what I want. Why's that? I prefer
to fight. But nothing is decided. I say again: 'If only you
were here.' Yet, if it becomes essential, I will send for
you. Anything else? Just this, I think. I am certain all
is lost. Why mince words any longer? But I write this
hurriedly and - believe me - in trembling. In future, I
shall write everything plainly to you, if I have a trustworthy
messenger, or else, if I write obscurely, you will understand all the same. In such letters I will call myself
Laelius and you Furius. The rest will be in riddles. Here
I am cultivating your uncle Caecilius and paying close
attention to him. I hear the edicts of Bibulus have been
sent to you. Our friend Pompeius is passionately upset
and angry at them.

Cicero, ad Atticum, II, xxi.

Rome. Between 25th July and 18th October 59.

1. On the state of the Republic, no need of great detail.
The Republic is completely lost, and in this respect more
distressed than when you left it; at that time there had
apparently overwhelmed the country a type of tyranny[5]
which was welcome to the masses and though irksome, at
least not deadly to loyalists[9]. However, it is now so
detestable to all that we shudder to think in what direction
it will erupt. For we have experienced the anger and
recklessness of those men; in their anger at Cato they have
destroyed everything. Even so they appeared to be using
such gentle poisons that it seemed we might die a painless
death. But now I am afraid that, what with the hissings of
the multitude, the talk of honourable men, and the murmur-

2. ings in Italy, they have become exasperated. For my part,
I hoped - as I used to tell you in our conversations and
regularly at that - that the wheel of state had turned in such
a way that we might hardly hear its sound, hardly see the

mark it had made in the ground. And so it would have
turned out, if people had been able to wait for the passing
of the storm. But having long sighed in secret, they
then began to murmur, and finally they all began to

3. speak out and actually complain aloud. So our dear friend
Pompey, not being accustomed to unpopularity, having enjoyed praise and glory in abundance, now physically disfigured and a mental wreck, does not know what direction
to take. In advance he sees a dangerous precipice, in
going back the charge of inconsistency. The loyalists
are opposed to him, the villains not his friends. Now see
how tender-hearted I am; I could not keep back my tears
when I saw him on the 25th July addressing a meeting of
the people about the edicts of Bibulus. In previous days
he usually carried himself so magnificently there, in that
supreme position, amid popular devotion and universal
support. How downcast and dejected he was then, how
unsatisfactory, not simply to the audience, but even in his

4. own eyes. What a sight! Crassus alone enjoyed it, no
one else. He had fallen from the stars, and so seemed to
have slipped rather than have gone of his own free will.
If Apelles should see his Venus, or Protogenes his famous
Ialysus, smothered in filth, each would, I imagine, feel
great pain. In the same way it was with deep sorrow that
I, who had painted and perfected this man with all the colours of my art now suddenly saw him disfigured. Though
none thought that I should be his friend on account of the
business with Clodius, such was my affection for him that
no injury could exhaust it. And so Bibulus' Archilochian
edicts against him are so agreeable to the people that we
cannot pass the place where they are posted for the crowds
of people reading them. They are so stinging to Pompeius
that he is wasting away with grief. I certainly find them
most annoying. They are excessively cruel to one for
whom I have always felt affection and I am afraid that being
so impulsive and keen to draw the sword, so unaccustomed
to insult, he may, with the full force of his feelings, give
free rein to his grief and anger.

5. I do not know what will be the end of Bibulus. As
things stand at the moment, he has a remarkable reputation.
Although he postponed the elections to the month of October,
Caesar had reckoned the meeting might be provoked by his
speech to march in protest to Bibulus' house, since altera-

tions of this kind are usually unpopular with the people. Though he made many inflammatory remarks, he could not raise a murmur. In short, they realise that no section of society supports them. All the more reason

6. for us to fear violence. Clodius is hostile to me, though Pompeius gives me an assurance that he will take no action against me. It is dangerous for me to believe him, and I am preparing to resist. I hope I will have full support from all classes. I miss you; moreover the situation calls for you to come and meet the crisis. If I see you in time, I will have at my side a great support in policy, morale, and actual defence. Varro is some help. Pompeius is an inspired speaker. I hope I will come out either with considerable honour or at any rate without inconvenience. Let me know what you are doing, how you are amusing yourself, and what dealings you have had with the people of Sicyon.

VII

FORCE AND FRAUD IN POLITICS

One of the main features of the history of the
last years of the republic is the use of more or less
organized violence in politics. Bribery and corruption were rife; Caesar's agrarian law was carried
'per vim', with the aid of Pompey's veterans; Clodius, Milo, and Sestius were all prominent in street
fighting; Cicero's house was destroyed and his brother's damaged; Pompey was jeered in the law courts
and mocked in the theatre; at Clodius' funeral the
mob burnt down the Senate House. The absence of
an effective police force is well known but cannot have
been the sole cause of the problem. Nor is it sufficient merely to point to the uses to which this violence
might be turned by political leaders. A.W. Lintott,
Violence in Republican Rome (Oxford, 1968), draws
attention to the extent to which popular notions of justice, involving the use of physical violence, received
official recognition in Roman law and underlay the
propensity to violence in politics. For the Roman
mob, the ordinary people of Rome about whom we
hear so little, see as background to this chapter P.A.
Brunt, The Roman Mob (Past and Present, 35, 1966)
and Z. Yavetz, The Living Conditions of the Urban
Plebs in Republican Rome (Latomus 17, 1958; reprinted in Seager, The Crisis of the Roman Republic
(Heffer, 1969).)

THE BONA DEA

The cult of the Bona Dea was confined to
women but in 62, when the festival was held in the
house of Caesar, P. Clodius Pulcher gained admit-
tance, disguised as a woman. In the ensuing scandal Caesar divorced his wife and Clodius was brought
to trial for sacrilege. Cicero disproved Clodius'
alibi and a conviction seemed certain until Crassus
secured an acquittal by bribing the jury.

Cicero, ad Atticum, I, xiv, 1-2 & 5

Rome, 13th. Feb. 61

1.   I don't want to bore you by saying how busy I am, but
all the same I am so distracted with work that I have scarce-
ly time even for this brief note, and must drop matters of
the greatest importance to write it.   I have already told you
what Pompey's first speech was like;   neither the poor nor
the well-off liked it, the revolutionaries thought it was futile
and the patriotic[9] found it lacking in dignity: in fact it fell
completely flat.   Then at the instigation of the consul Piso,
Fufius, an utterly worthless tribune, brought Pompey forward to speak to the people.   (All this was happening in the
Flaminian Circus, and there was a bank holiday crowd there
that day).   He was asked whether he thought the jury should
be chosen by the praetor, and that the same praetor should
use them as advisers, this being the proposal adopted by the
2. senate in the case of Clodius' sacrilege.   Then Pompey replied in a rather high and mighty way, saying that he thought
the authority[1] of the senate of the greatest importance in
all matters and that he had always done so - all this at some
length.   Later the consul Messalla asked Pompey in the
senate what he felt about the sacrilege, and the bill which
had been introduced.   Pompey's reply took the form of a
speech praising all the decrees of the Senate in general
terms, and he said to me as he sat down that he thought his
answer even covered the events of my consulship.

5.   As for the situation in Rome, the Senate is excelling
itself in firmness, strictness and courage - a real Areo-
pagus.   For when the day came for submitting the Senate's
proposal to the people, the young men with their fancy little
beards turned up in force, all Catiline's gang in fact, under
that pansy Curio, and asked the people to reject the bill.
Besides, Piso, the consul who had proposed the bill, was
himself against it.   Clodius' thugs manned the gangways,
and the voting tablets were given out in such a way that
.everyone received a rejection tablet.   At this point - you
really should have been there - Cato jumped on to the platform and gave Piso a startling telling-off, if that is the word
to describe a speech that breathed nothing but dignity, nothing
but authority[1] and, in a word, nothing but good sense.
Even our friend Hortensius joined him, and many good men[9]
besides;   indeed Favonius' efforts were outstanding.   When
the optimates rallied like this, the Comitia Centuriata were

dismissed, and the Senate was summoned. A full house
passed the decree, instructing the consuls to urge the people
to accept the proposal; Piso strenuously opposed it, and
Clodius fell in entreaty at the feet of every single person;
only about fifteen voted with Curio, who was for making no
decree at all, and there were easily four hundred against
him. That settled the matter, and the tribune Fufius then
gave way. Clodius made some pitiful remarks in which he
attacked Lucullus, Hortensius, Gaius Piso and the consul
Messalla with insults; he accused me only of "being in the
know" about everything. The Senate then proceeded to pass
a resolution to stop all business concerning the praetors'
provinces, and the reception of ambassadors, and so on,
until the bill became law.

Cicero, ad Atticum, I, xvi, 1-5.

Rome, July 61

1.   You ask me what can have happened about the trial that
its end was so completely unexpected, and you also want to
know why I showed less fight than usual. I shall answer you
by starting at the end, as Homer does. For as long as I had
to defend the senate's authority[1] I battled with such energy
and vigour that the crowd cheered me on and I covered myself
with glory. Indeed, if you have ever thought me a brave
politician, you would certainly have applauded my performance in this case. For when Clodius took refuge in speeches,
in which he used my name to stir up hatred, by heavens, how
I fought! What destruction I spread around me! How I laid
into Piso, Curio and all that gang! How I blasted the flippan-
cy of the older men and the indecency of the youth! Many
was the time, believe me, when I longed to have you here,
not only to support my plans, but also so that you could see
2. how splendidly I fought. But then Hortensius had the idea
of putting up the tribune Fufius to bring in a bill about the
sacrilege, which only differed from the consular proposal on
one point, namely the class of people who were to make up
the jury - and of course this was the crucial point, - and
struggled hard to get this passed, because he had already
persuaded himself and others that no jury would every acquit
Clodius. I gave up the fight, for I saw how hard up the jury
was, and gave no evidence at all, except what was already so
well known and attested that I could not pass over it. So if
you want to know why he was acquitted, to answer your first

60

question, the reason was the empty pockets and itching palms of the jury. Moreover we have the advice of Hortensius to blame for this disaster, for he was afraid that Fufius would veto the measure which was being proposed in accordance with the decree of the senate and completely failed to see that it would have been far better to leave Clodius in disgrace and obliged to appeal for pity, than to entrust the matter to a weak jury. But instead he was led by his hatred to pre-cipitate the trial, saying that even a sword of lead would cut his throat.

3.　　　If you want to know what the actual trial was like, I can tell you at once - it had an amazing ending. Right from the start I disapproved of Hortensius' plan, and now after the event so does everyone else. The rejection of jurors took place amid vociferous shouting: the prosecutor, like an up-right censor, was rejecting all the depraved characters, while the defendant, like an indulgent promoter of gladiators, was putting on one side those who were men of integrity. Once the jurors took their seats, decent citizens[9] began to lose all confidence. You've never seen a shadier set of characters sitting down together, even in a third-rate night-club; there were senators with a mark against their name, bankrupt equites, treasury officials hunting for treasure. There were still a few decent citizens[9] there, whom Clodius hadn't managed to eliminate by rejection; they sat there gloomy and dispirited among this incongruous company and were obviously worried that the ill-repute of their neighbours

4. might spread to them. During the preliminaries, as various matters were referred to the jurors for decision, their strict-ness and unanimity were astonishing. The defendant failed in all his requests, and the prosecutor obtained even more than he asked for. As you can imagine, Hortensius was delighted with his unique foresight; everybody thought that Clodius was not just on trial but had already as good as been condemned a thousand times. When I went forward to give my evidence, I'm sure you must have heard the noise Clo-dius' supporters made as the jurors rose to protect me, demonstratively offering their own throats to save my life. I took this as a much greater compliment than when your fellow-Athenians refused to allow Xenocrates to take the oath before giving evidence or when our Roman judges re-fused to examine the accounts of Metellus Numidicus when

5. they were being carried round in the usual way. Yes, a much greater compliment. And so, when the jurors hailed

me as the saviour of their country, the defendant was shattered, and all his patrons with him. The next day the crowd that came to meet me was as large as the crowd that escorted me home at the end of my consulship. Then our splendid Areopagites shouted that they wouldn't come to court unless they were given a bodyguard. The question was put to the court, and there was only one man who didn't vote for a bodyguard. The matter was referred to the Senate; a decision was reached, expressed in ponderous, elaborate words; the jurors were commended, and the magistrates were entrusted with the task of providing a bodyguard. Nobody imagined that Clodius would put up any defence.

"Now tell me, Muses, how the fire first fell." You know Baldhead, from the Nanneian set, my trumpet-blower whose flattering speech about me I've already mentioned to you. In two days, with the help of one slave, and an ex-gladiator at that, he'd sewn up the whole business: invitations, promises, offers of security, outright gifts. And on top of their pay some jurors were even given nights with certain ladies or introductions to young men of noble family; it really is a shocking affair. Most of the decent citizens[9] left and the Forum was full of slaves, but there were twenty-five jurors stout-hearted enough to prefer death to dishonour, though their danger was clear enough. Thirty-one thought more of their pockets than of their reputations. When Catulus saw one of them, he said "Why did you ask us for a bodyguard? To get your money home safe?" There, as briefly as I can put it, is the sort of trial it was and that's how Clodius was acquitted.

THE EXILE OF CICERO

Two years later Clodius was elected tribune for 58 and at once began to attack Cicero on the grounds that he had executed the Catilinarians without trial and had thus infringed a Lex Sempronia of C. Gracchus which asserted the right of the people to be the final judge in all capital cases involving a Roman citizen. Once in office Clodius proposed a bill to outlaw anyone who had killed a Roman citizen without trial. Cicero may have hoped that his acts were protected by the passage of the Senatus Consultum Ultimum in October 63. Like other senatorial decrees this had no legal force, but it represented the corporate opinion of the Senate and thus possessed immense auctoritas. This

had previously been sufficient to protect those who
had operated under it, though the trial of Opimius in
121 and Caesar's prosecution of Rabirius in 63 show
that the manner, at least, of its implementation had
been questioned. The desire of the Triumvirs to
see Cicero removed from the political scene in Rome
and the collapse of the concordia ordinum on which
he had so prided himself in 63 left Cicero dangerously
exposed to attack and in March 58 he yielded to pressure and went into voluntary exile. A bill outlawing
him was passed immediately after, in the Concilium
Plebis. Within a year the situation had changed; the
consuls of 57 were more favourable to Cicero, two of
the tribunes, Milo and Sestius, worked actively for
his recall, and Pompey himself had been sufficiently
alarmed by Clodius' activities to back their efforts.
Early in August a bill was passed through the Comitia
Centuriata and a month later Cicero was back in Rome.
(For Cicero's political aims on his return see Ch. IV,
Cicero, pro Sestio, 96 - 105)

Cicero, pro Sestio, 75 - 79

75.   While the resolution[1] of the Senate was being delayed
by every kind of hindrance, trickery and subterfuge, the day
for discussing my case in the Plebeian Assembly, January
25th, finally arrived. Fabricius, the proposer of the motion
for my recall and a very good friend of mine, took over the
rostrum a little before dawn. Sestius, who is here now
accused of violence, remained quiet on that day: this ad-
vocate and champion of my case did nothing, awaiting my
enemies' first moves. And what of the men who have planned Sestius' prosecution in this court, how were they beha-
ving? In the dead of night, they took over the forum, the
comitium, and the Senate house with armed men (most of
whom were slaves); then they attacked Fabricius and laid
violent hands on him, killing several people and wounding
76. many others in the process. Marcus Cispius, that most
loyal and upright tribune of the people, was also attacked
as he was entering the forum and was driven from it. Then,
after causing the greatest bloodshed in the same place, with
drawn and bloody swords they began to search every corner
of the forum, shouting for my brother, my most excellent,
brave and devoted brother. The latter, in his great sorrow
and longing for me, would gladly have offered his body to
their weapons - not to fight back, but to die - had he not

preserved his life in the hope of witnessing my return home.
Yet, he did not altogether escape the criminal attacks of
this band of hooligans: although he had only come to plead
with the Roman people for the safety of his brother, he was
driven from the rostrum and forced to lie low in the comitium, hiding behind the bodies of slaves and freedmen and
guarding his life not with the mantle of the law and justice,
77. but with the cloak of darkness and flight. You yourselves,
jurors, doubtless recall how the river Tiber was filled with
the bodies of citizens, how the sewers were choked, and
how the blood was wiped up from the forum with sponges;
in fact, people came to believe that this huge force, this
splendid array of men belonged, not to a private citizen and
a plebeian, but to a patrician and a praetor.

Yet neither previous to this occasion nor on that rio-
tous day itself did you charge Sestius, gentlemen. 'But
still, there was violence in the forum' some one may say.
Certainly there was, and when greater? We have often
seen stone-throwing and not so often, but still too often,
drawn swords: but who has ever witnessed such terrible
bloodshed, such piles of corpses in the forum, except perhaps on the day when Cinna and Octavius fought each other?
A riot often starts when a tribune imposes his veto in a
stubborn and uncompromising spirit, or because of a cul-
pable or unscrupulous proposal brought forward to secure
some advantage or gain for the politically naive, or from
some rivalry between magistrates; but such a riot arises
gradually, first with shouting, then by a division of opinion
at a meeting, but only rarely and late in the day do men resort to blows. Who has ever heard of a riot erupting in
the middle of the night, without a word being spoken, without a meeting being called, without any law being proposed?
78. Is it likely that any Roman citizen, any free born man at all,
would go down into the forum before daybreak sword in hand
to prevent the proposal of my recall - except those who are
urged on by that plague-ridden and accursed Clodius and
have long since been gorging on the life blood of the state?

Here I now ask his accuser, who complains that during his tribunate Sestius was surrounded by a large crowd
of guards, whether he was so guarded on that day in question. Indeed he was not. As a result the cause of the
state was defeated, and defeated not by omens, not by a
tribune's veto, not by a free vote, but by force, violence,
the sword. For, if that praetor who claimed that he had

observed bad omens in the sky, had blocked Fabricius'
proposal, then the state would have suffered a setback, but
a setback such as it could have endured; if Fabricius'
colleague had interposed his veto, then he would have done
harm to the state, but done harm by right of his tribune's
authority.   But what right do you have, Clodius, to send
your gladiators in before dawn - gladiators assembled in
expectation of your receiving the aedileship - together with
murderers discharged from prison?   What right do you
have to expel the magistrates from the rostrum, to cause
great bloodshed, and to clear people out of the forum? And,
when you have done all this by force of arms, what right
have you to accuse this man, who surrounded himself with
a bodyguard, not to attack you, but merely to be in a position to defend his own life?

79.   Yet even after then Sestius took no steps to be protected by his friends and thus be able to carry out the various
duties of his office safely in the forum.   He put all his
trust in his sacred position as tribune and, believing that
the laws protecting his sanctity made him safe not only
from physical violence but even from interruptions and
abuse, he went to the temple of Castor and reported to the
consul that the omens were unfavourable for public business.   Suddenly the Clodian gang, with many bloody victories over our citizens already to its credit, interrrupted
him, caused a disturbance, and attacked him.   Sestius
was unarmed and caught off his guard as some attacked
him with swords, others with pieces of the wooden railings
or with clubs.   Severely wounded, his body hacked about
and weakened by loss of blood, he threw himself to the
ground as though dead;   what saved his life was only the
fact that they thought him already dead.   When they saw
him lying there, lifeless and exhausted, cut to pieces and
at his last gasp, they eventually stopped striking him - not
through any sense of pity, but more through weariness and
the mistaken belief that he was no more.

Cicero, ad Atticum, IV, i

Rome, Sept. 57

1.   When I first came to Rome and there was a man to
whom I could safely entrust a letter, I thought that before
I did anything else I should write and thank you, since you
can't be here, for your help in the matter of my recall.

65

To be quite honest, I came to the conclusion that you had shown no more courage or good sense than I, and that, considering my past attentions to you you had not been particularly energetic in trying to save me from exile; and yet I also discovered that you, who had at the beginning of the crisis shared my miscalculations - say rather my panic - and echoed my mistaken fears, had been bitterly hurt by our separation and had put all your resources, enthusiasm,

2. energy and efforts into securing my recall. So I can truthfully say that at this moment, when the joy and happiness I longed for have all come about, there is only one thing needed to crown it; to see you and embrace you properly. And once I do get you here, see if I let you go again! I intend to claim all the arrears of your delightful friendship that are owing me from the past, and if I don't, I shall consider that I don't really deserve my good fortune in being brought back from exile.

3. As for my political position, I thought it would be difficult for that to be re-established; but so far I have recovered my public distinction, my prestige[1] in the Senate and my popularity among all the good citizens, more completely than I had thought possible: but about my personal property, (and you know how that has been damaged, broken up, and stripped bare) I am in considerable difficulties. I really need you, not so much for your resources which I'm sure are at my disposal, as for your advice in collecting and reassembling what is left to me.

4. Now, although I think your friends have written in detail about it all or that you may have heard reports or rumours, all the same I'll describe briefly what I think you would particularly like to hear from my pen. On August 4th I left Dyrrachium - the same day that the Bill for my recall was passed. The next day I reached Brundisium. There was my darling Tullia to meet me, on her birthday - a happy coincidence that it was also the foundation day of the colony of Brundisium and of the temple of Prosperity which stands near your house; the coincidence was noticed by the townsfolk and was celebrated with great popular delight. On the 11th, still at Brundisium, I had a letter from Quintus saying that the law had gone through the Comitia Centuriata, amid overwhelming enthusiasm from all age-groups and classes and supported by a great flock of voters from towns all over Italy. So after I had been treated with great favour and

respect at Brundisium I set off for Rome, and on the way
deputations came to congratulate me from all around.

5. When I finally got to Rome, my arrival was such a triumph
that everyone known to my nomenclator, of whatever social
class, came to meet me, except for those of my personal
enemies who had no chance to disguise or deny their hostility.   When I reached the Porta Capena the steps of the
temples were crowded with the common plebeians, who
cheered and applauded to show their delight;   the same sort
of cheering crowds fêted me as far as the Capitol, and
unbelievable numbers in the Forum and on the Capitol itself.

Next day in the Senate, September 5th, I made my
formal speech of thanks.

6.   Two days afterwards the price of corn had rocketed;
crowds had demonstrated first at the theatre, then at the
Senate, shouting at Clodius' instigation that the shortage of
corn was all my fault.   A debate was held in the Senate
about the matter;   everyone, not just the plebs but respectable citizens[9] as well, was shouting for Pompey to be
put in charge of ensuring supplies;   Pompey himself wanted
it, and the crowd was calling on me by name to propose it,
so I did so in a carefully worded speech.

Since all the consulares except Messalla and Afranius
had absented themselves, with the excuse that it would be
unsafe for them to speak, a decree was passed on my motion,
"that discussions be held with Pompey with a view to his
taking special responsibility for the situation, and that he
be legally empowered to do so."   When the decree was
read and the people had applauded in this new and vulgar
way we have at the mention of my name, I made a speech,
on the invitation of all the magistrates present except one
praetor and two tribunes.

7.   The day after, a packed Senate with all the consulares
present gave Pompey everything he asked for.   When he
asked for fifteen legates, he named me as the chief and
said I should be his alter ego in all matters.   The consuls
drafted a bill to give Pompey complete responsibility for
the corn-supply for five years, in all countries: Messius
produced an alternative which gives him complete financial
powers, throws in a fleet and an army and authority[4] in

67

the provinces to override even the governors. The proposal from me and the consuls now looks quite reasonable,
Messius' intolerable. Pompey says he wants ours, his
friends say that he prefers Messius'. The consulares
are furious, following Favonius' lead; I'm keeping rather
quiet, particularly since the religious authorities have
still not given an official reply about my house. If they
invalidate Clodius' consecration, I shall have a fine site
and the consuls will assess compensation for the building
as the Senate has decreed they should: if they don't, they
will at least pull down Clodius' building and contract for
a new one under their name, not his; in that case they
will assess compensation for both site and building for me.

8.   So that's how things are; sometimes they seem good,
sometimes bad - it depends on my attitude at the time. I
am, as you know, rather worried about my financial position. There are also some family matters which I prefer
not to put in a letter. Quintus my brother has shown his
loyalty, courage and devotion to me, and I love him for it
as I should. I am longing to see you; do come quickly,
and come prepared to give me your best professional advice; it's as though I were beginning my life all over
again. Already some of those who supported me when I
was in exile are beginning, now I've returned, to show
open jealousy and ill-concealed anger. I need you badly

MORE RIOTING

In 57 Milo wished to prosecute Clodius for
violence but was prevented by the latter's election
as curule aedile for 56. In 56 Clodius instituted
a prosecution of Milo for violence, but the case
was later dropped and Milo was elected praetor
for 55.

Cicero, ad Atticum, IV, iii

Rome, 23rd Nov. 57

1.   I'm sure you're anxious to know what's happening here
and to hear my own news from me; not, of course, that
what happens in public is better reported by me than by
anyone else who might write to you or tell you about it;
but you will see from my letters what my own reaction to

events is, what state of mind I'm in, and how I stand in general.

2.   On the 3rd of November, the workmen were driven off the site of my house by armed men, and the portico of Catulus, which is being rebuilt under consular contract by decree of the Senate and had almost reached roof level, was broken down. First they damaged my brother Quintus' house by throwing stones at it from my property, then they set fire to it at Clodius' orders and threw burning pieces of material at it in sight of the whole city, to the accompaniment of lamentation and complaints, I won't say of all decent people[9], since I'm not sure whether there are any, but of just about the whole population. Clodius himself rushed around raving, and after this display of madness seemed obsessed with killing his enemies; he went from street to street, openly inciting slaves to revolt and gain their freedom. On a previous occasion, when he managed to avoid a trial, he had a difficult case - he was obviously guilty - but at least he did have one; he could deny the charge, divert it on to other people, even claim some kind of legality for his actions. But after this devastation, arson, and rapine he has been deserted by his followers, and barely retains the support of Gellius or the undertaker Decimus; he relies on the advice of slaves now, and realises that if he openly murders anyone he wants, his case when he gets to court will be no worse than it is already. As a result,

3. I was chased by him and his men as I went down the Sacred Way on November 11th: shouts, stones, sticks, swords, and all without any warning! I retreated to Tettius Damio's entrance hall, and my companions kept his gangs out with ease. Clodius could have been killed, but I'm tired of the surgeon's methods, and am changing to a more gentle treatment. But when he saw that everybody was crying out not for his trial, but for his immediate punishment, he made the Catilinae look as respectable, in retrospect, as the Acidini. On 12th November he tried to storm Milo's house - the one on the north-west slopes of the Palatine - and burn it; he made his attempt in broad daylight, at eleven in the morning, accompanied by men with drawn swords and shields and others with lighted torches; he had taken over Publius Sulla's house as his headquarters for the attack. Then Quintus Flaccus led a vigorous sortie from Milo's family house, the Anniana, killed the most notorious of Clodius'

mob of brigands, and wanted to give Clodius himself the same treatment, but he escaped into the interior of Sulla's house. Then on the 14th the Senate met; Clodius stayed at home; Marcellinus was admirable, everybody full of determination. Metellus began a well-organised filibuster, abetted by Appius and even by that friend of yours, of whose resolution and excellence your letters have spoken so truly. Sestius was mad with anger. Clodius threatened reprisals against the city if he didn't get his elections. Marcellinus then proposed his motion, which he read from written notes so as to cover the whole of my case - the building-site, the burnings, and the danger I was in - and made sure that all this would be dealt with before Clodius' elections: whereupon Milo declared that he would observe the skies on all

4. the days on which elections could be held. Then we had more speeches: Metellus tried to stir up trouble, Appius was reckless, Publius was simply lunatic. The end result was that the elections would have been held, but for Milo's observing unfavourable omens in the Campus Martius. On November 20th he entered the Campus before midnight with a large crowd of supporters at his heels: Clodius didn't dare enter the Campus, even though he had a select band of escaped slaves at his disposal. Milo stayed there till noon the next day, to his great honour and amid a wonderful display of joy on the part of the populace. The struggle that the three brothers had put up was disgraceful; their strength was broken; their frenzied actions viewed with contempt. But now Metellus insisted that next day Milo's observation of the heavens must take place in the Forum; there was no point, he said, in Milo's coming to the Campus by night, for he himself would be in the Comitium at seven in the morning. What happened was that on the 21st, Milo entered the Comitium before sunrise. As dawn broke, Metellus began to hurry secretly through back streets to the Campus: Milo intercepted him between the groves on the Capitol and declared unfavourable omens. Metellus beat a retreat, while Quintus Flaccus hurled scornful vulgarities at him. The 22nd was a market day; there were no meetings on that or the following day.

5. I am writing this on the 23rd, at three in the morning: Milo is already in possession of the Campus Martius. My neighbour, Marcellus, who is standing for aedile, is snoring audibly. I am told that Clodius' entrance hall is deserted save for a few ruffians and a cheap lantern. His supporters claim that all this is my doing, not knowing the

bravery and generalship of our hero Milo. His courage is admirable. The news I'm sending you is a rare delight; now to sum up. I don't think the elections will be held, and I think Milo will bring Clodius to trial - if he doesn't kill him first, - for I can see Milo killing him with his own hands if they run into one another in a crowd. He has no qualms about this; in fact he boasts about it and isn't put off by what happened to me. After all, he won't rely on the envious and treacherous for advice, nor trust a feeble noble.

My mind is active, even more than when I was at the peak of my career, but my property is diminished. I am repaying my brother Quintus' generosity as far as I can afford, and now that he refuses my money so as to stop me going bankrupt, I am appealing to my friends for help. Without you here, I'm not sure what to do in general about my affairs; so do hurry up and come.

Cicero, ad Quintum fratrem, II, iii, 1-4

Rome, 12th Feb. 56

1.   I wrote to you before about events up to the time of my last letter; now listen to what has happened since. The reception of the provincial delegations was put back from 1st February to 13th February. Business was not finished on the 1st. On the 2nd Milo stood his trial. Pompey came to defend him, and Marcellus spoke for him at my request; we came out with flying colours, and the case was postponed until 7th February. In the meantime, although the deputations had been put off till the 13th, dis- cussion started on the provinces for the quaestors and the Treasury votes for the praetors; but since there was so much disquiet on the state of the nation nothing was settled. C. Cato tabled a bill to remove Lentulus from his governor- ship[4]. His son put on mourning.

2.   On 7th February Milo was up for trial. Pompey spoke - or rather wanted to; for as soon as he got up, Clodius' gangs created an uproar and kept it up throughout his speech, interrupting it not just with heckling, but with all kinds of insult and abuse. When he had finished (he certainly stood up to the occasion and was not dismayed; he said all he had to say, on occasion even without inter- ruption, when his prestige[1] won him a hearing); anyway,

when he had finished, Clodius rose to his feet. There
was such an uproar from our side at this (for we had
decided to return the compliment[8]) that his composure
was upset and he could control neither the tone of his
voice nor the expression on his face. This state of affairs
continued until nearly one o'clock, although it was hardly
eleven o'clock when Pompey had finished, with all sorts of
abuse against Clodius and Clodia culminating in obscene
verses. He was white with fury and in the midst of the
shouting called on his supporters to say who it was who was
starving the common people to death. His gangs answered,
"Pompey". Who wanted to go to Alexandria? "Pompey",
they answered. Who did they want to go? "Crassus"
they answered. (He was there at the time and certainly
wasn't at all friendly towards Milo). About two o'clock,
as if at a signal, Clodius' supporters began to spit on ours.
Tempers were fierce. They tried to move us out. Our
men took the offensive, his gangs were put to flight,
Clodius was thrown off the platform; and then I too took to
my heels so as not to get caught in the riot. The Senate
was called into session. Pompey went home. I have not
been to the Senate, because I would either have to keep
quiet about such serious events or in defending Pompey
offend some loyal citizens[9] (for he was being taken to
task by Bibulus, Curio, Favonius and the younger Servilius.)
The whole matter was put off until the next day. Clodius
gave notice of postponing the trial till the festival of the
Quirinalia.

3.   On 8th February the Senate met in the temple of
Apollo to allow Pompey to be there, and Pompey made an
impressive speech. But nothing was decided that day. On
9th February at the temple of Apollo a Senatorial decree
was passed to the effect that events on 8th February were
subversive. That day C. Cato weighed in heavily against
Pompey and through his whole speech levelled accusations
at him as if he were standing in the dock; about me he
spoke at great length in the most fulsome praise - though
much against my will; when he began to upbraid Pompey
for disloyalty towards me, he was heard out in utter silence
by my opponents. Pompey replied to him in strong terms,
alluded to Crassus, and declared openly that he would take
more care to protect his life than Africanus had done when
4. C. Carbo had murdered him. Then I reckoned that events
were already building up to a climax. For Pompey is well
aware, and has confided to me, that plots are being hatched

against his life, that C. Cato is backed by Crassus, that
Clodius is being supplied with funds, that both of them are
being pushed both by him and by Curio, and by Bibulus and
the rest of Pompey's detractors; we must take great care
that he is not overwhelmed by the alienation of the dema-
gogue-fed populace, by the hostility of the nobility, by the
prejudice of the Senate and by the unscrupulousness of the
young men. So he is taking precautionary measures, and
calling men up from the country; while Clodius is stiffen-
ing his own gangs; a group is being prepared for the
festival of the Quirinalia. Milo's forces already make us
far the stronger party for that occasion, but a large band
of reinforcements is also expected from Picenum and the
'ager Gallicus'; so we should also be able to resist Cato's
proposals about Milo and Lentulus.

THE END OF THE GANGSTERS

In January 52 Clodius was murdered in a brawl
on the Appian Way between his gang and Milo's. His
body was brought back to Rome for cremation in the
forum and in the process the Senate House was burnt
to the ground. As had happened also a year earlier,
rioting had made it impossible to hold the elections
in 53 - Milo was standing for the consulship and Clodius for the praetorship of 52 - and the year opened
without any magistrates in office. The SCU was
passed and shortly afterwards Pompey was elected
'sole consul'. Milo was brought to trial in April,
was convicted, and went into exile at Marseilles.

Cicero, pro Milone, 24-29

24.   Publius Clodius had decided to spend his praetorship
harassing the state by every sort of criminal action; but
he realised that, since last year's elections had dragged on
for so long, his own period of office would only last a few
months. He was not anxious, as other men are, to gain
higher rank; he wanted to avoid having as his colleague
that outstanding citizen Lucius Paullus. Even more, he
wanted to be able to devote a whole year to the disruption
of the state. This is why he suddenly gave up the chance
of being elected praetor in the first year in which he was
eligible and waited till the next year. Not for him the
religious scruples which sometimes lead men to do this;

his object, as he used to admit himself, was to get a full, uninterrupted year for his praetorship - that is, for the over-
25. throw of the state. What worried him was that his praetorship would be severely inhibited if Milo was consul in the same year; and he realised that Milo would, in all probability, be elected consul by an overwhelming majority of the Roman People. And so he attached himself to Milo's rivals for the consulship and made sure he was running their campaigns, whether they liked it or not. The result was, as he was fond of saying, that he carried the whole election on his own shoulders: he marshalled the tribes, intervened personally in the arrangements, and enrolled the equivalent of a new Colline tribe from the dregs of the population. But the more Clodius tried to create confusion, the stronger Milo's position grew from day to day. Eventually Clodius realised, not just from gossip but on the basis of votes cast at meetings of the Roman People, that this bravest of men, his own most determined enemy, was certain to be elected consul. Clodius did not intend to stop at anything: he brought his movements out into the open, and declared
26. publicly that Milo should be killed. He now brought down from the Appennines gangs of rustic, barbarous slaves whom he had used to ravage the forests and to harass Etruria - you have often seen them. He made no secret of what he was up to; in fact, he several times said publicly that Milo's consulship could not be taken from him, but his life could. He often made statements to this effect at meetings of the Senate, and said as much at mass meetings; and when the gallant Favonius asked him what he could hope to gain from all this violence while Milo was alive, he replied that in three days, or four at the outside, Milo would be dead. Whereupon Favonius promptly came and told Marcus Cato here what he had said.

27.   Meanwhile, Clodius had discovered (not that it was hard to find out from the citizens of that town) that Milo was travelling to Lanuvium on January 20th; this journey was required by the obligations of law and ritual, for Milo was chief magistrate of Lanuvium, and had to proclaim the new high priest there. Having discovered all this, Clodius suddenly left Rome the day before, with the intention, as events showed, of ambushing Milo in front of the Clodian country estate. His departure meant that he was unable to attend a turbulent mass meeting held on that day, at which his characteristic violence was badly missed. In fact, we can be sure that he would not have missed it, had he not

been anxious to be on time at the place arranged for the
28. ambush. Meanwhile Milo was at a meeting of the senate.
When it ended, he went home, changed his shoes and tunic,
waited a while (as men usually do) while his wife got ready,
then set off at about the time when Clodius could have
returned to Rome - had he intended to come back that day.
But Clodius was lightly equipped when he met him, riding
not in a carriage but on horseback; he had no baggage to
get in his way, none of the Greek companions with whom he
usually travelled, and - very unusual, this - was even without his wife. Milo here, who is accused of making the
journey deliberately and openly to kill Clodius, was muffled
up in a heavy cloak and was riding in a carriage with his
wife; he was accompanied by a large, heavily-laden,
feminine and unwarlike cortège of maidservants and page-
boys.

29.   And so at about four o'clock in the afternoon he was
confronted by Clodius in front of the latter's country seat.
At once, a large body of armed men charged straight at him
from higher ground, killing his coachman as they went.
Milo, however, threw back his cloak, leapt from the carriage,
and began defending himself with vigour. Clodius' followers
now had their swords drawn; and while some moved round
the carriage to take Milo in the rear, the others, thinking
he had already been killed, began to kill his slaves, who had
been following behind. Some of the slaves who were loyal
to their master and acted with determination were killed;
others, who saw that there was fighting around the carriage
but were unable to reach it to help Milo, were told by Clodius that he was dead, and believed it. These slaves of
Milo's without the knowledge or command, or even the
presence, of their master - I say this openly, not to divert
any charge that may be laid, but just as things happened -
did just what any of us would have wanted his slaves to do
in similar circumstances.

Asconius, in Milonianam, pp. 39-42C.

34.   Then witnesses were called according to the law which,
as I mentioned before, decreed that before the case proper
witnesses should be heard for a period of three days. The
jurors should then seal the testimony of the witnesses and
on the fourth day they should all be ordered to attend and in
front of the accuser and defendant the balls on which the
names of the jurors were inscribed should be made of equal

size and shape. On the following day 81 jurors should be chosen by lot, and should then immediately go into session. The accuser should then have two hours for speaking, the defendant three, and the case should be decided on that same day. Before a verdict was reached, however, the accuser and the defendant should each reject five jurors out
35. of each of the three orders forming the jury, leaving 51 jurors to record their vote.

On the first day there was presented as witness against Milo one C. Causinius Schola. He stated that he had been with P. Clodius when he was killed and did all he could to emphasize the atrocity of the crime. When M. Marcellus began to question him, he was so intimidated by the extent of the disturbance caused by the Clodian supporters present that, fearing a murderous assault, he took refuge with Domitius on the tribunal. For this reason Marcellus and Milo himself begged Domitius to protect them. At this time Cn. Pompeius was sitting near the temple of Saturn, where the Treasury was situated, and had been disturbed by that same uproar. He therefore promised Domitius that he would come to the court on the next day with a body of armed men. This he did. Subdued by this, Clodius' supporters allowed the evidence of the witnesses to be heard in silence for the remaining two days. The witnesses were interrogated by M. Cicero, M. Marcellus and Milo himself. Many of the inhabitants of Bovillae gave testimony about the events which had taken place there - the innkeeper had been murdered, his inn broken into, and the body of Clodius dragged out into the open. In addition the Alban Virgins stated that an unknown woman had come to them at Milo's bidding to discharge a vow because Clodius had been killed. The last to give testimony were Sempronia (the daughter of Tuditanus and the mother-in-law of P. Clodius) and Clodius' wife Fulvia. By their display of tears they greatly disturbed those who were present. When the court was dismissed about four o'clock in the afternoon, T. Munatius publicly exhorted the people to attend in large numbers on the following day. He adjured them not to let Milo escape and to make sure that the jurors who passed them on the way to the court should realize their opinion and see the indignation they felt. On the next day, which was the last of the trial, 7th April, the
36. shops were closed throughout the entire city. Pompeius stationed guards both in the forum and at every entrance to it, while he himself, as on the previous day, seated himself

in front of the Treasury in the midst of a select body of troops. The selection of jurors from the first day was now made. Afterwards there was as much silence in the forum as could be expected in any such place. Then between seven and eight in the morning the accusers began to speak, the elder Appius, M. Antonius, and P. Valerius Nepos. They made full use of the two hours permitted by the law.

In reply there was only one speaker, M. Cicero. Now some people wanted the defence against this charge to take the form of a plea that Clodius' death had been in the interest of the state – this was the line that M. Brutus took in the speech which he composed on Milo's behalf and published as if he had delivered it. Cicero, however, did not agree, maintaining that it should not be possible even for a man whose conviction was in the interests of the state to be killed without a trial. So when the accusers put forward the allegation that Milo had planned an ambush for Clodius – falsely, for the brawl had arisen by chance – Cicero seized on the point and taking the opposite view asserted that it was Clodius who had set an ambush for Milo. In fact the whole of his speech revolved around this interpretation of the facts. But the generally agreed version of the story was as I have said: that the fight had occurred on that day without any planning on either side, that the meeting had in fact been accidental, starting as a mere brawl between the slaves and ending with the murder of Clodius. However, it was a well-known fact that they had often threatened one another with death and though the fact that Milo's retinue was larger than Clodius' made Milo suspect, Clodius' retinue had been travelling with less luggage and was thus better prepared for a fight. When Cicero began to speak, he was confronted by the shouts of Clodius' supporters who refused to keep quiet even with the threat of the soldiers standing around them. As a result he did not speak with his usual self-possession. The speech which Cicero actually delivered on this occasion still survives, but the one which he later wrote – and on which I am commenting – is so perfect that it can justly be placed in the first class.

VIII

THE CIVIL WAR

The Conference of Luca in 56 put an end to the hopes Cicero had entertained since his return from exile that the power of the Triumvirate might be broken by detaching Pompey from the alliance and winning his support for a revived concordia ordinum. (See Ch. IV, Cicero, pro Sestio, 96 - 105.) The conference arranged for an extension of Caesar's Gallic command and for second consulships and subsequent provincial commands for Pompey and Crassus. The power of the Triumvirate seemed yet more firmly established.

In 54, however, Julia died; as Caesar's daughter and Pompey's wife she had formed the only bond of personal affection between the two. In 53 Crassus, whose desire to match Caesar and Pompey as a general had led him to insist on a major military command as his province, was killed fighting the Parthians at Carrhae. These events, his need to insure his position against Caesar's return from Gaul, and his seemingly genuine concern at the collapse of public order in Rome both brought Pompey closer to the Optimates and made him more acceptable to them. In 52 Pompey married Cornelia, the daughter of Metellus Scipio, who became his colleague in the consulship for the last five months of the year.

Thereafter, the determination of Caesar's opponents in the Senate to recall him as soon as possible and to prosecute him immediately he was out of office, the advantage Pompey gained over Caesar by the extension of his Spanish command for a further three years, and Caesar's refusal to surrender his command, and thus his army, before he could safe-guard his position by election to a second consulship led through the political manoeuvres of 51 and 50 to the outbreak of the Civil War in January 49. (For the problems connected with the date of Caesar's return from Gaul, see J.P.V.D. Balsdon, JRS, 29, 1939 and P.J. Cuff, Historia, 7, 1958.)

Cicero, ad familiares, VIII. viii. 4-10.

Rome; from Caelius to Cicero, Oct. 51.

4.   As for state affairs, expectation of developments in
the two Gauls has put a stop to business for many days now;
eventually, however, after frequent postponement the problem has been seriously discussed and it has become quite
clear that Pompey inclines to the view that a decision for
Caesar's recall should be taken after March 1st.   Here
is the decree of the Senate and the resolutions[1] it
recorded.

5.   "Decree of the Senate, and resolutions[1]: drafted
on 30th September in the temple of Apollo by L. Domitius
Ahenobarbus, son of Cnaeus, of the tribe Fabia, Q. Cae-
cilius Metellus Pius Scipio, son of Quintus, of the tribe
Fabia, L. Villius Annalis, son of Lucius, of the tribe
Pomptina, C. Septimius, son of Titus, of the tribe
Quirina, C. Lucilius Hirrus, son of Caius, of the tribe
Pupinia, C. Scribonius Curio, son of Caius, of the tribe
Popilia, L. Ateius Capito, son of Lucius, of the tribe
Aniensis, M. Eppius, son of Marcus, of the tribe Terentina.   In accordance with the proposals of M. Marcellus,
consul, about the provinces to be assigned to those who
had held the consulship, it was resolved as follows: that
the consuls elect, L. Paulus and C. Marcellus, shall,
when they have entered office, after the 1st March of their
year of office, bring a motion before the Senate about the
provinces to be assigned to those who had held the consulship; that after the 1st March they shall bring no other
motion before the Senate prior to or in conjunction with
the above; that for this business they may hold meetings
of the Senate during the elections and may pass a decree
of the Senate, and, when the matter is brought before the
Senate, it may be permitted them without risk to summon
from their duties those who are in the number of the
three hundred judges; that if there is need to refer the
matter to the people or plebs, the consuls of the present
year, Ser. Sulpicius and M. Marcellus, the praetors, and
tribunes of the plebs, such as may be appointed, shall
refer the business to the people or plebs; but that, if
they have not referred it, whoever succeeds them shall
do so. This decree was passed.

6.   Drafted on 30th September in the temple of Apollo by
L. Domitius Ahenobarbus, son of Cnaeus, of the tribe Fabia,
Q. Caecilius Metellus Pius Scipio, son of Quintus, of the
tribe Fabia, L. Villius Annalis, son of Lucius, of the tribe
Pomptina, C. Septimius, son of Titus, of the tribe Quirina,
C. Lucilius Hirrus, son of Caius, of the tribe Pupinia, C.
Scribonius Curio, son of Caius, of the tribe Popilia, L.
Ateius Capito, son of Lucius, of the tribe Aniensis, M.
Eppius, son of Marcus, of the tribe Terentina.   In accordance with the proposals of M. Marcellus, consul, about the
provinces, it was resolved as follows: that the senate considers that those who possess the power to impose the veto,
or to obstruct the business of the Senate should not cause
a delay which might make it impossible for a motion concerning the political interests of the Roman people to be brought
before the Senate with all speed or for a decree of the Senate
to be passed;   that any attempt to prevent or delay public
business is considered treasonable by the Senate.   If anyone
imposes a veto on this decree of the Senate, the Senate resolves that its resolution[1] be recorded and that a motion
on this subject be brought before the Senate at the first
opportunity.   C. Caelius, L. Vinicius, P. Cornelius, C.
Vibius Pansa, tribunes of the plebs, imposed their veto on
this decree.

7.   The Senate also resolves with regard to the soldiers
who are in the army of C. Caesar that those of them who
have completed their service or have other reasons why they
should be discharged shall be referred to this order for
their claims to be considered and their cases to be investi-
gated.   If anyone imposes a veto on this decree of the Senate,
the Senate resolves that its resolution[1] be recorded and
that a motion on this subject be brought before this order at
the first opportunity.   C. Caelius, C. Pansa, tribunes of
the plebs, imposed their veto on this decree.

8.   The Senate also resolves with regard to the province
of Cilicia and the eight remaining provinces which ex-
praetors hold with a praetor's authority that those who have
been praetors and who have not held authority[4] in a province but have a claim under a decree of the Senate to govern
provinces with a praetor's authority[4] should be appointed
to these provinces by lot: that if of that number who ought
to proceed to the provinces by a decree of the Senate the
required number to set out to those provinces is not found,
then, in accordance with the seniority of each praetorian

college, those who have not set out for provinces shall thus set out for provinces assigned to them by lot: that if these do not make up the required number, then those of the college next in order who have been praetors and who have not set out for provinces shall be included in the allotment until the number is reached that is required for despatch to the provinces. If anyone imposes a veto on this decree of the Senate, the Senate's resolution[1] shall be recorded. C. Caelius and C. Pansa, tribunes of the plebs, imposed their veto on this decree."

9.   The following remarks of Pompey were also noticed and produced a widespread feeling of confidence. He declared that it would be wrong for him to settle the question of Caesar's provinces before 1st March, but that after that date he would not hesitate to do so. When questioned about the possibility of a veto on that occasion, he said that it made no difference whether Caesar openly disobeyed the Senate's wishes or arranged for someone to impose his veto on the Senate's decision. "But what," asked another, "if he wants both to be consul and to keep an army?" What a forbearing answer he gave: "What if my son wants to beat me with a stick?" This reply led to the general belief that Pompey was negotiating with Caesar. And so now, as I see it, Caesar is willing to consent to one or other of these two conditions: either he stays where he is and his candidature is not accepted for this year: or, if he can be

10. elected, he withdraws from his province. Curio is making himself quite ready to oppose him. I don't know what the outcome can be; however, I do see that Curio has the right opinions and cannot really fall even if he achieves nothing.

Cicero, ad Atticum, VII, ix.

Formiae, 26th. or 27th. Dec., 50.

1.   You ask me if you should expect a letter from me every day. The answer is 'yes' - if I can find a courier. If you say that I am virtually home now, my answer is - I shall stop writing only when I actually get there. It seems that there is one of your letters I have not received, the one that my friend Lucius Quinctius was carrying when he was

2. wounded and robbed at Basilus' tomb. Please see whether there was anything in it that I ought to know, and at the same time please decide this political problem for me.

There are the following possibilities:-

(1) that the notice of Caesar's candidature is accepted and he keeps his army with the authority of the Senate or of the tribunes of the plebs;

(2) that he is persuaded to surrender his province and army and become consul in this way;

(3) that, if he is not persuaded to do this, elections are held without accepting his candidature, and that he accepts the situation and keeps his province;

(4) that, if he does not accept the situation and makes use of the tribunes' veto but makes no further move, the out-come is an interregnum;

(5) that, if he brings in his army because his candidature is not accepted, we shall have to use force to resist him.

In any event, Caesar will be the first to use force and he may do this (a) immediately, when we are less well pre-pared, or (b) at the elections, when his friends' demand for the acceptance of his candidature according to the law of the Ten Tribunes is rejected. Moreover, he may have recourse to arms (a) for the single reason that his candida-ture is not accepted or (b) for the additional reason that some tribune of the plebs, while obstructing the Senate or egging on the people, may have been censured or have had his power curtailed by a decree of the Senate or have been suspended or removed from office or, claiming to have been thus removed, have fled for refuge to Caesar. Once the war starts, either (a) the city must be held or (b) it must be abandoned, and in that case it will become necessary to cut Caesar off from food and all other supplies. Of all these evils, one of which must certainly be endured, you must decide which you think the least.

3.   Of course, your answer will be - for him to be persua-ded to surrender his army and to become consul in this way. If he is prepared to accept it, this is certainly a course to which no exception can be taken, and I am surprised at his not acting thus if he does not obtain permission to stand and to retain his army. Some people, however, think that we need fear nothing more than to have Caesar as our consul. "But", you will say, "I prefer it thus than with an army." Certainly, but that "thus" of yours is considered a great

disaster by someone, and it's one for which he has no cure.
"We must yield, if that is his wish." Imagine a second
consulship of his, after what you saw of the first one. "He
was comparatively weak then, but even so he had more power
than the whole state." So what do you think he will be like
now? If Caesar is consul, Pompey has decided he must be
in Spain. What a wretched business! for the worst possibility is the one that cannot be rejected, and yet, if he took
this course, he would immediately become popular[8] with
all the decent citizens[9].

4.   Disregard, then, this course; according to Pompey,
Caesar cannot be brought to accept it. Which is the next
worst? To yield to his demand, which Pompey says is utterly shameless. What could be more so? You have held
a province for a period of ten years, granted you not by the
Senate, but by yourself through violence and intrigue. The
time set, not by the law, but by your own fancy, is up; but
assume it was by law. Your succession is decreed; **you**
obstruct and say "accept my right to stand." You accept
our rights! Are you to keep your army longer than the
people ordered and against the Senate's wishes? "You will
have to fight, if you don't give in." Let us reply in the
words of Pompey, that we shall fight with good hope of
victory or of death in freedom. When we fight, if fight we
must, is a matter of chance, and our strategy depends on
circumstances. However I won't trouble you with that
problem. Give me any views you have about my remarks.
As for me, I am on the rack, day and night.

Caesar, Civil War, I, 1 - 7.

1.   The consuls received the despatch from Caius Caesar
but only reluctantly agreed to it being read before the Senate
under extreme pressure from the tribunes. Even so, they
could not be persuaded to allow the contents of the despatch
to be put to debate, holding instead a general debate on
matters of state. The consul Lucius Lentulus promised
that he would not fail the republic and the Senate if that body
were fearless and forthright in its declaration of policy, but,
if it followed its former course of appeasement towards
Caesar and tried to win favour[8] with him, he would allow
self-interest to dictate his policy and would take no notice of
any expression of the Senate's opinion[1]; they should
remember that he too had claims upon Caesar's favour[8]

and friendship. Scipio spoke in the same vein; he said that Pompey would not fail the republic provided the Senate supported him; if it hesitated now and did not act with sufficient determination, there would be little point in the senators' changing their minds later and then asking for
2. Pompey's help. Because this meeting of the Senate was being held inside the city and Pompey was near at hand, it seemed that Scipio was acting as his mouth-piece in this speech.

Some had expressed a more moderate opinion. For example, Marcus Marcellus embarked on a speech to the effect that it was not a good idea to put a motion before the Senate on the issue until levies had been held throughout Italy and armies raised. With these for protection the Senate would then be bold enough to carry any resolution it liked, in safety and without duress. Again, there was Marcus Calidius who proposed that Pompey should remove any cause for war by setting out for his provinces. He maintained that Caesar was afraid that Pompey was holding on to the two legions which he had taken from him and was keeping them at Rome to threaten his security. Marcus Rufus, who followed Calidius, took substantially the same line. All three senators were taken to task and severely censured by Lentulus, who declared categorically that he would not put Calidius' proposal; Marcellus was alarmed by the consul's savage criticism and withdrew his opinion. In this way, the harangues of the consul, the fear of a nearby army, and the threats of Pompey's friends coerced the majority of the Senators into unwilling acceptance of Scipio's resolution: namely, that Caesar disband his army by a day to be determined; failure to comply with this resolution would result in his being treated as a public enemy. The tribunes Marcus Antonius and Quintus Cassius imposed their veto. There was an immediate debate on the tribunician veto, and harsh measures were advocated. In fact, the applause of Caesar's enemies rose in proportion to the savagery and cruelty of the views which the various speakers expressed.

3. Towards evening the Senate was adjourned and all the members of that body were summoned out of the city by Pompey. The determined received his praise and encouragement for the future, the waverers were rebuked and spurred to action. From all quarters many soldiers from the former armies of Pompey were called out, lured by the prospect of rewards or promotion, and many too were

summoned from the two legions surrendered by Caesar. The city, the slope leading up to the Capitol, and even the Comitium were crowded with military tribunes, centurions, and recalled veterans. The consuls, Pompey, and those who maintained old feuds with Caesar mustered all their friends and adherents in the Senate. This vociferous gathering intimidated the weaker senators, rallied the hesitant, and actually made it impossible for the majority to exercise their right to a free vote.

The censor Lucius Piso and Lucius Roscius, a praetor, offered to go to Caesar to inform him of these events and asked for a period of six days for the accomplishment of this task. Several expressed the opinion that envoys be sent to Caesar to put before him the Senate's decision.

4.   All these proposals encountered stubborn resistance from the speeches of the consul Lentulus, Scipio, and Cato. Cato was motivated by his long-standing feud with Caesar and by vexation at his defeat in the consular elections. Lentulus, who was deeply in debt, hoped to obtain a provincial command with an army and bribes from kings seeking official recognition; indeed, among his friends he boasted that he would be a second Sulla and that the supreme power[4] would fall to him. Scipio was spurred on by the same prospect of a province and an army command; grounds of kinship, he considered, would entitle him to share these with Pompey; at the same time he feared prosecution in the law courts; he was susceptible to the flattery of certain powerful men who at the time had great influence in political affairs and in the law courts; his own vanity and that of these men was a further motive. Pompey himself was driven on by Caesar's enemies and by his determination that no-one should equal his own prestige[2]. He therefore broke with Caesar and was restored to favour[8] with those who had once been the common enemies of Caesar and himself. Yet the vast majority of these enemies he himself had imposed upon Caesar when he had contracted a marriage alliance with his daughter Julia. He was also influenced by the discredit he had incurred in the matter of the two legions; they had been intended for service in Syria and Asia, but Pompey had turned them into a private army designed to support his own unconstitutional position[5]; he was thus eager for open war.

5.   For these reasons all transactions were carried out in an atmosphere of haste and disorder. Caesar's friends

were given no time to inform him of these events. The
tribunes of the plebs had no opportunity of protesting at the
threat to themselves or even of retaining, by the exercise
of their veto, their most basic rights - which even Sulla
had left them -, but were compelled to take thought for their
personal safety only seven days after coming into office.
In former times even the most violent tribunes had not cus-
tomarily to worry about the consequences of their various
acts until at least eight months had passed. Recourse was
had to the senatus consultum ultimum, which had never previously been proposed even by the most headstrong senators
except when the city was virtually on fire and there was a
total collapse of public confidence. It runs as follows: the
consuls, praetors, tribunes, and proconsuls who are in the
vicinity of the city are to ensure that the state suffers no
harm. The decree was dated 7th January. Thus it was
that the first five days available to the Senate for meetings
since the commencement of Lentulus' consulship - two days
had been taken up by business in the Comitia - witnessed the
most harsh and hostile decrees regarding Caesar's command[4] and the position of the tribunes. The latter at once
left Rome and made their way to Caesar. He was at Ravenna,
awaiting a reply to his very moderate demands and hoping
that some sense of human justice might make a peaceful
settlement possible.

6.   During the following days the senate met outside the
city. Pompey's policy was the same as he had indicated
through Scipio. He praised the courage and loyalty of the
Senate and revealed the strength of his own forces, declaring that he had ten legions in a state of readiness. Moreover he had it on good authority that Caesar's soldiers were
dis-affected and could not be persuaded to defend or follow
him. Proposals on outstanding matters were put at once to
the Senate, namely that a levy be held throughout Italy, that
Faustus Sulla be sent without delay to Mauretania, and that
money from the treasury be granted for Pompey's use.
There was a further proposal that King Juba be given the
title "ally and friend" but the consul Marcellus refused to
allow this for the present. The tribune Philippus blocked
the proposal regarding Faustus Sulla, but the other proposals
were incorporated in senatorial decrees.

        The provinces, two consular and the remainder prae-
torian, were allotted to private citizens. Scipio obtained

Syria and Lucius Domitius, Gaul.   Under a private arrange-
ment Philippus and Cotta were passed over, their lots not
being included in the ballotting.   Men of praetorian rank
were sent to the remaining provinces.   They did not, in
accordance with the practice of previous years, wait for
their commands[4] to be confirmed by the people, but depar-
ted in military attire after offering the usual vows.   The
consuls left the city, something which had not happened before that time; and private citizens were attended by lictors
in the city and even on the Capitol, though this was quite
contrary to all ancient practice.   Levies were held throughout Italy, weapons were requisitioned, money exacted from
the municipalities and carried off from the temples, without
regard for the distinction between divine and human.

7.   When Caesar was informed of these events he addres-
sed his assembled troops, reminding them of the injuries he
had always suffered at the hands of his enemies.   These
enemies, he complained, had alienated Pompey from him
and led him astray, by jealously belittling his own merits
although he had always strongly supported Pompey's position
and reputation[2].   He went on to lament that a new precedent had been set in the state now that the tribunes' power
of veto, recently restored by force of arms, was being
criticized and even suppressed by force of arms.   Even
though Sulla had stripped the tribunician power of everything
else, he had at least left the power of veto intact.   Pompey,
however, who had the credit for having restored those
powers which the tribunes had previously lost, had now
taken away even what they had previously retained.   Caesar
declared that the decree instructing the magistrates to ensure that the state came to no harm - the decree by which
the Senate called the Roman people to arms - had never been
passed except at times of harmful legislation, tribunician
violence, or popular insurrection when the temples and the
heights commanding the city had been seized by the plebs.
These precedents from an earlier age had been made good
by the deaths of Saturninus and the Gracchi.   But on this
occasion none of these actions had even been contemplated,
far less undertaken.   Under his leadership, they had in
nine years conferred the greatest fortunes on the state, won
countless victories, and pacified the whole of Gaul and
Germany, and he urged them now to defend his good reputation and standing[2] from his enemies.   The soldiers of the
Thirteenth Legion, which was on the spot - Caesar had
summoned it at the outbreak of the crisis, but the rest of

his legions had not yet arrived -, shouted their assent and declared their readiness to avenge the wrongs done to their general and to the tribunes of the plebs.

Cicero, ad Atticum, VII, xi, 1

Campania;   January, 49.

What, I ask, is this?   What is happening?   I am quite in the dark.   "We hold Cingulum", people say, "we have lost Ancona;   Labienus has deserted Caesar."   Are we talking of a Roman general or of Hannibal?   Oh mad and wretched man!   he has never seen even the Shadow of the Good.   And he says that he has done all this for the sake of his reputation[2].   But what sort of a reputation can a man have without honourable conduct?   Is it honourable to have an army without a commission from the state, to make his advance on his own city easier by capturing towns inhabited by Roman citizens, to set about confiscations of property, recalling exiles, and hundreds of other crimes, - and all "to grasp the greatest of the goddesses, Tyranny"?   Well, much good may it do him.   I would rather have one day basking in your sun, which is free to all, than all that sort of kingship[6], and would rather die a thousand times than let that sort of thought once enter my head.

Cicero, ad Atticum, VIII, iii.

Cales, Feb. 18th, 49.

1.   I am in a turmoil of worry on a very important issue and there is no possibility of talking things over with you, yet I wish to have the benefit of your advice.   The crux of the whole matter is this: if Pompey should leave Italy, as I rather think he will, what do you consider that I should do? To help you to make up my mind for me, I will set down briefly the arguments which occur to me on either side.

2.   All that Pompey did for my own welfare (which was a very great deal) and my friendship with him, - but even more than this, patriotism too, would seem to point to the conclusion that Pompey's policy should be my policy, his cause mine.   There is an additional consideration.   If I stay, and cut myself off from that company of reliable and distinguished citizens which follows Pompey, then inevitably I shall fall into the hands of one man.   He is a man, it is

true, who does much to make clear his goodwill towards me (and as you yourself know, I took care long ago to ensure that he should feel goodwill, having some inkling of this storm which threatens us), yet two points call for reflection. Firstly, how far is he to be trusted? Secondly, even if fully reassured about Caesar's goodwill, can a man of courage and a loyal[9] citizen stay in a city in which he has held the highest offices and authority[4], has great achievements to his credit, and was raised to a venerable priesthood, if it means that he will not be the man he was, and if he must run the risk of disgrace should Pompey ever recover political control? These are the arguments on the one side.

3.   Now look at the arguments on the other side. Not one of our friend Pompey's actions has been well-advised; not one has been courageous; and, incidentally, on every single occasion he has flouted my counsel and ignored the influence[1] that my advice ought to carry. I am not referring to the old, well-worn facts, that it was he who fostered, and promoted, and supported Caesar's political career, he who was responsible for the forcible carrying of Caesar's laws in defiance of the auspices, that it was he who increased Caesar's province by the addition of Further Gaul, who became his son-in-law, who sanctioned as augur the adoption of Publius Clodius into the plebeians, he who was more zealous to end my exile than he had been to prevent it, he who extended Caesar's provincial command and in Caesar's absence from Rome promoted his interests in everything, he who, even in his third consulship when he had begun to uphold law and order, exerted his influence on the ten tribunes to propose that Caesar's candidature should be accepted in his absence and expressly sanctioned this provision by a law of his own and opposed the consul Marcus Marcellus when he was trying to set 1st March as the limit of Caesar's tenure of the Gallic provinces. All this I will pass over, but what could have been more shameful, what more irrational than this departure from Rome - or, to describe it more accurately, this disgraceful flight? Would it not have been better to accept any terms rather than be forced into abandoning the fatherland? The terms were stiff, I grant you, but could anything be worse than this?

4.   He will win back his political hold, you say? When? What step has been taken to encourage that hope? Picenum has been lost. The way to Rome stands open. All the

money in the capital, both public and private, has been handed over to the opposing party. In short, there is no watchword, there is no backbone, there is no rallying point for those who would like to see the constitution defended. Apulia has been chosen, the most thinly populated district of Italy, furthest from the vital theatre of this war. It seemed as though, in his despair, the chance of flight which the seaboard offered was Pompey's sole consideration. I assumed the command at Capua unwillingly, not because I wished to shirk such a responsibility, but the cause was one for which there was no enthusiasm from the senatorial and equestrian orders and no openly expressed private concern – it is true that responsible citizens[9] did to a certain extent feel themselves involved, but only in their usual lukewarm way – and I felt that the great mass of the people and certainly all the humblest were inclined towards the

5. other side, many of them eager for revolution. I therefore told Pompey that I would undertake nothing without a garrison and without money. So I have had no responsibility at all, because from the beginning I saw that his only intention was flight. If I make that my intention now, where shall I go? I cannot join Pompey. When I set out towards him I learnt that Caesar was in that region, so that I could not safely reach Luceria. I shall have to embark on the Tuscan sea for an unknown destination in the depths of winter. Well, then, shall I take my brother with me or just my son? Either course will entail very great difficulty and very great anxiety, and what an onslaught Caesar will make on me and on my fortunes when I have gone – a fiercer one than he will make on others because he will think, perhaps, that in doing violence to me he has a means of recommending himself to the populace. Then, too, these shackles – the fasces, I mean, these emblems of my triumphs – what a problem it is to transport them out of Italy! But even supposing that the sea is calm for me, where shall I find safety until I can reach Pompey? Yet I'm ignorant of the route to take and even of the destination.

6. But if I stay behind and find a niche on Caesar's side, I shall have acted as Lucius Philippus and Lucius Flaccus and Quintus Mucius acted during Cinna's tyranny[5] – no matter how, in the event, things turned out for Mucius. He used to say that he foresaw his fate but that he would rather have it so than march in arms upon his fatherland. Thrasybulus chose a different and possibly a nobler course. But Mucius's line of reasoning and his point of view are thoroughly sound, and so are those of Philippus, to suit one's

action to the circumstances when one must and to let no
opportunity slip when it is offered. Even in this solution
of the dilemma these fasces of mine present a problem.
Assume that Caesar will be well-disposed, which is by no
means certain, but assume it. He will offer me a triumph.
Not to accept it - that could be dangerous: to accept - that
could drive a wedge between me and the Pompeians[9]. A
knotty, insoluble problem, you will say ! Yet solved it
must be. What can possibly be done? Perhaps you will
think me more inclined to stay because my arguments for
that solution have been lengthier. It may be, however, as
often happens in the courts, that one side is wordier, the
other has more fact. So you see that I am calmly weighing
up a question of the utmost gravity and I should like to have
your advice. I have a ship ready in the harbour at Caieta
and one at Brundisium too.

7.   But what do you think? As I actually write these
words by night in my house near Cales - messengers arrive.
A despatch is brought to me with the news that Caesar is
before Corfinium, and that Domitius is in Corfinium with
an army which is steadfast and eager to fight. I do not think
that our Gnaeus will go so far as to abandon Domitius, although he has sent Scipio on ahead to Brundisium with two
cohorts and has written to the consuls that in his opinion the
legion enrolled by Faustus Sulla should be taken to Sicily by
one of them. But it will be a shocking thing to abandon
Domitius when he is crying out for help. I have some hope,
not a great deal to be sure, but in this neighbourhood it is
regarded as well-founded, that Afranius has fought an engagement with Trebonius in the Pyrenees and that Trebonius
has been routed, that your Fabius, too, has deserted with
his cohorts. My very greatest hope, however, is that
Afranius is approaching with large forces. If so, perhaps
I will stay in Italy. However, since there are doubts about
Caesar's route, because he is thought to be going to march
perhaps towards Capua or perhaps towards Luceria, I am
sending Lepta to Pompey with a despatch, and I myself am
returning to Formiae, so as not to run into any trouble.

I wanted you to know all this, and my mind is now
more composed than when I wrote a little while ago. I am
asking you to make a decision without putting forward my
own.

Cicero, ad Atticum, VIII, xi, 2.

Formiae; 27th. February, 49.

Our friend Pompey has never been of this mind, and least of all nowadays. He and Caesar have both aimed at absolute power[5], and not with the idea of making the state happy and renowned. Pompey has left the city, but not because it could not be defended, and Italy, but not because he was driven out. No, from the outset he has intended to raise a storm on every land and sea, to rouse to war the kings outside our borders, to lead their savage tribes in arms against Italy, and to build up huge armies. That sort of rule[6], the rule[6] of a Sulla, has long been his aim, and many of those who are with him also desire it. Do you think that there was no possible common ground, no chance of a compromise between him and Caesar? The opportunity is still present even today. But neither of them makes our happiness his aim. They both want to be master[6].

Cicero, ad Atticum, VIII, xiii

Formiae, 1st March, 49.

1.   You can take my secretary's handwriting as proof of the inflammation of my eyes; that is also why I shall be brief - though at this moment there is nothing for me to tell you. I am entirely taken up with waiting for news from Brundisium. If Caesar catches up with our good Pompey, there is a faint hope of peace; if Pompey gets across first, we must fear a ruinous war. But do you see what sort of man he is, into whose power the republic has fallen - how shrewd, how active, and how well-prepared? If he doesn't kill anyone and doesn't deprive anyone of anything he will certainly be most devotedly adored by those

2. who had been most afraid of him. The men of the munici- pia and country districts talk to me a good deal: they have absolutely no regard for anything beyond their lands, their miserable estates, and their wretched cash-boxes. Look how the situation has been turned upside down! They fear the man whom they formerly trusted, adore the man they used to fear. I cannot contemplate without anguish the failures and faults on our side which have brought about this result. But I have written to tell you what I think is in store, and I now wait to hear from you.

Cicero, ad Atticum, VIII, xvi

Formiae, 4th March, 49.

1.   I have made all my arrangements, apart from a secret and safe journey to the Adriatic: at this time of year I can't set sail from the west coast. But what route do I take to get to where my thoughts are turned and where events call me? For I must go and quickly, in case I am hindered or held back by any circumstance. It is not the Great Man who draws me on, as you imagine; I knew him long since to be the most useless of statesmen, but now I see that he is also the most useless of generals. No, it is not he that draws me, but the things men are saying - as reported to me by Philotimus. He alleges that the optimates are tearing me to shreds. You gods! what optimates! - look at the way they are now running to meet Caesar, trying to ingratiate themselves with him! The country towns look on Caesar as a god - it's not just pretence, as it was when they offered up prayers for Pompey

2. when he was ill. Clearly, any harm that this Pisistratus refrains from doing will earn him as much gratitude as if he had stopped someone else doing it. They hope that Caesar can be placated; Pompey, they believe, is enraged. Imagine the crowds that come flocking from the towns to meet Caesar, imagine the honours that are paid him! "They are afraid of him", you will tell me. Doubtless they are, but they are far more afraid of Pompey, believe me. Caesar's specious clemency delights them, while they dread Pompey's resentment. Those jurors who were on the panel of 360, who used to be particularly pleased with our friend Pompey, - and I see one or another of them every day - are terrified of certain threats Pompey made at Luceria. So I would like to know who these 'optimates' are, to turn me out while they remain at home. And yet, whoever they are, "I fear the Trojans". Nevertheless I see what prospects I am setting out with; I am joining a man who is more ready to devastate Italy than to win a war and I await a tyrannical master[5]. And indeed, as I write to you on the 4th I am even now waiting to hear something from Brundisium. But what do I mean by "something"? I mean news of Pompey's cowardly flight from there, and the route and destination of Caesar's triumphant return. When I have heard this, I am thinking of going to Arpinum, if Caesar comes up the Appian Way.

IX

CAESAR'S DICTATORSHIP

The office of dictator had been established in the early years of the republic, being employed in crises of exceptional severity. Dictators were appointed in the Senate, and their term of office lasted for not more than six months. In this form the dictatorship was not employed after the Second Punic War, but in 82 Sulla revived the office in a new form, becoming dictator 'to pass laws and settle the affairs of the state' (legibus scribundis et reipublicae constituendae) and remaining in office for two years. Caesar was first appointed dictator in 49, remaining in office for only eleven days to conduct the elections; in 48 the appointment was for a year; in 46 for ten years; and in 44 for life.

Between January 49 and October 45 Caesar was almost wholly engaged in fighting the Pompeian armies, visiting Rome only in the brief intervals between one campaign and the next. In the last six months of his life he was preparing to mount an expedition against the Parthians. This makes it hazardous to draw conclusions as to what Caesar's later policy might have been, had he survived, from his administrative measures during this period. Even so two features, of personality rather than policy, stand out: his practical and detailed interest in a wide range of administrative problems - calendar, corn-supply, debt, elections etc. - and his impatience with the constitutional traditions of the republic.

Suetonius, _Divus Julius_, 40-44.

40. Turning next to the regulation of home affairs, he reformed the calendar which had long been rendered so chaotic by the failure of the pontiffs to be systematic in their intercalation that the harvest and vintage festivals did not fall in summer and autumn respectively; and he made the year conform to the course of the sun, giving it a total of 365 days; he abolished the intercalary month and intercalated one day every fourth year. To ensure in future that his method of dating should start running smoothly from the 1st January following, he inserted in the current year two other

months between November and December; and the year in which these arrangements were made totalled 15 months including the intercalary month, which in accordance with previous practice had also been inserted that year. He

41. brought the Senate up to full strength, created new patricians, and increased the number of praetors, aediles, and quaestors, and even of the minor magistrates; he reinstated those stripped of their rank by the action of the censors and those convicted of bribery in the criminal courts. He shared with the people the responsibility for electing magistrates, in such a way that, except in the case of the consulship, the successful candidates for office were half elected by the people and half nominated by himself. He published the names of his candidates in brief notices sent to the various tribes: "Caesar the dictator to tribe X; I commend to you A and B, that your votes may enable them to achieve the high office they deserve(2)." He allowed even the sons of the proscribed to hold office. He reduced the classes composing the juries in the criminal courts to two, the equestrian and senatorial, removing the tribuni aerarii, who had formed the third class. He revised the census list of citizens, but used a new method, and did not hold it in the usual place; he made the landlords of tenement blocks fill in the register for their respective streets. He reduced the numbers of those receiving the corn dole from 320,000 to 150,000; and to avoid the need to summon fresh meetings whenever the register needed revision, he ruled that every year the praetor should select by lot some of those not on the register to fill the gaps caused by death.

42. 80,000 Roman citizens were sent to various colonies outside Italy. All this drained away the population of the city of Rome and to maintain numbers there also, he passed a law that no Roman citizen between the ages of twenty and (fifty) and not on active service should be absent from Italy for more than 3 years at a time, and that no senator's son should travel abroad except on the staff or in the retinue of a magistrate; and that owners of ranches should recruit at least one third of their cattlemen from free-born adults. He bestowed Roman citizenship on all doctors and teachers of liberal studies at Rome, to encourage them to settle there and to make others eager to join them. As regards debts he disappointed expectations, which had frequently been encouraged, of a general cancellation, but finally decreed that debtors should give their creditors appropriate satisfaction after a valuation had determined the price paid for their various possessions before the civil war. Any interest paid

in cash or by banker's pledge was to be deducted from the principal, a regulation which cancelled roughly a quarter of the debts remaining. He disbanded all clubs except those of ancient foundation. He increased the penalties for crime; and since the well-to-do found it all the easier to indulge in crime because exile did not cost them their family estates, he deprived murderers of near relatives, as Cicero tells us,

43. of all and other criminals of half their property. He dispensed justice with great thoroughness and great rigour. He went so far as to expel from the senate men convicted of extortion. He annulled the marriage of an ex-praetor, who had married a woman only two days after she had been divorced from her previous husband, although there was no suspicion of adultery. He introduced customs dues on imported goods. He made it illegal to ride in a litter, and also to wear crimson garments and pearls except for certain specified people and age-groups and on specified days. He made a point of enforcing the law against extravagance, posting guards at various points around the market, to confiscate and convey to him forbidden delicacies; sometimes he secretly despatched lictors and soldiers to enter a dining-room and remove any such delicacies that his guards had failed to notice, even if they were already on the table.

44.   He entertained designs, which daily grew more numerous and ambitious, for improving the appearance and amenities of the city, and also for the protection and expansion of the empire: in particular he planned to build a temple to Mars, larger than any other existing temple, (though this would have involved filling up a lake on which he had previously staged an exhibition of naval warfare, and then levelling the surface), and to build a colossal theatre nestling against the Tarpeian Rock; to codify civil law, and from the vast and diffuse body of laws to select the best and indispensable ones and concentrate them in a very few volumes; to provide the public with the largest Greek and Latin libraries possible, giving Marcus Varro the task of collection and classification; to reclaim the Pomptine marshes and to drain the Fucine Lake; to build a road from the Adriatic across the range of the Apennines as far as the Tiber; to drive a canal through the Isthmus of Corinth; to curb the Dacians, who had poured into Pontus and Thrace; and shortly to invade Parthia through Armenia Minor but to conduct a thorough reconnaisance before launching hostilities.

     Such were his activities and projects when death cut him short.

Cicero, ad familiares, VII, xxx

Rome, Jan. 44; to M' Curius

1.   I no longer urge or even ask you to return home; indeed my own wish is to rush away from here and go to some spot 'where I may hear neither the name nor the deeds of the descendants of Pelops'. I consider my behaviour unbelievably disgraceful, in taking part in this business. Really, you were, I think, far quicker to foresee the danger threatening, getting out of Rome at the time you did. These events may be painful to hear about, but it is far worse actually to see them. At least you were not there in the Campus Martius, when the elections for the quaestorship started about 8.00 a.m. and the official chair was in position for Quintus Maximus, whom Caesar's supporters claimed was consul; but when Maximus' death was announced, the chair was removed. Then Caesar held a meeting of the Comitia Centuriata, although it was for the Comitia Tributa that he had taken the auspices; shortly after midday he proclaimed as consul a man who was to hold office until the First of January, which was the following morning. So you'll realise that no one had lunch when Caninius was consul. Still no disasters were suffered in his consulship; he showed astonishing vigilance, for in his entire consul

2. ship he never had a wink of sleep. You find this a huge joke; well, you aren't here. If you were, you too would be bound to cry. Suppose I tell you the rest of the news? There are incidents beyond number of the same kind; which I can only endure by taking shelter in the haven of Philosophy and having my dear Atticus to accompany me in my studies. You write that you are his property by right of ownership and obligation, and mine by use and enjoyment. I don't object; what a man enjoys and uses is really his. But more of this at another time.

3.   Acilius, who has been sent to Greece with the legions, is very much in my debt (I defended him twice, when conviction would have meant exile, and on both occasions got him off); he is a very grateful fellow, and treats me with great deference. I have written him a very detailed letter about you, and have enclosed it with my letter to you. Please write and tell me his reaction to it and any promises he makes to you.

80 L. Cornelius Sulla Felix II; Q. Caecilius Metellus Pius
79 P. Servilius Vatia; Ap. Claudius Pulcher
78 M. Aemilius Lepidus; Q. Lutatius Catulus
77 D. Iunius Brutus; Mam. Aemilius Lepidus Livianus
76 Cn. Octavius; C. Scribonius Curio
75 L. Octavius; C. Aurelius Cotta
74 L. Licinius Lucullus; M. Aurelius Cotta
73 M. Terentius Varro Lucullus; C. Cassius Longinus
72 L. Gellius Poplicola; Cn. Cornelius Lentulus Clodianus
71 P. Cornelius Lentulus Sura; Cn. Aufidius Orestes
✳ ── 70 Cn. Pompeius Magnus; M. Licinius Crassus
69 Q. Hortensius; Q. Caecilius Metellus Creticus
68 L. Caecilius Metellus; Q. Marcius Rex
67 C. Calpurnius Piso; M' Acilius Glabrio
66 M' Aemilius Lepidus; L. Volcacius Tullus
65 L. Aurelius Cotta; L. Manlius Torquatus
64 L. Iulius Caesar; C. Marcius Figulus
63 M. Tullius Cicero; C. Antonius
62 D. Iunius Silanus; L. Licinius Murena
61 M. Pupius Piso Calpurnianus; M. Valerius Messalla Niger
60 Q. Caecilius Metellus Celer; L. Afranius
59 C. Iulius Caesar; M. Calpurnius Bibulus
58 L. Calpurnius Piso Caesoninus; A. Gabinius
57 P. Cornelius Lentulus Spinther; Q. Caecilius Metellus
Nepos
56 Cn. Cornelius Lentulus Marcellinus; L. Marcius Philippus
✳ ── 55 Cn. Pompeius Magnus II; M. Licinius Crassus II
54 L. Domitius Ahenobarbus; Ap. Claudius Pulcher
53 Cn. Domitius Calvinus; M. Valerius Messalla Rufus
52 Cn. Pompeius Magnus III; Q. Caecilius Metellus Pius
Scipio
51 Ser. Sulpicius Rufus; M. Claudius Marcellus
50 L. Aemilius Paulus; C. Claudius C.f. Marcellus
49 C. Claudius M.f. Marcellus; L. Cornelius Lentulus Crus
48 C. Iulius Caesar II; P. Servilius Vatia Isauricus
47 Q. Fufius Calenus; P. Vatinius
46 C. Iulius Caesar III; M. Aemilius Lepidus
45 C. Iulius Caesar IV (without colleague);
    Q. Fabius Maximus; C. Trebonius;
    C. Caninius Rebilus
44 C. Iulius Caesar V; M. Antonius;
    P. Cornelius Dolabella

INDEXES

a) Roman proper names

(listed alphabetically under the most commonly used name)

C. Porcius CATO (Tr Pl 56)   71, 72, 73
M. Porcius CATO (Uticensis) (Q 64?, Tr Pl 62, Q propr
    Cyprus 58-6, Pr de repetundis 54, Promag Sicily
    & Greece 49-8, Propr in Africa 47-6) 36, 51, 55, 59, 74, 85
Q. Lutatius CATULUS (Cos 102) 69
Q. Lutatius CATULUS (Pr by 81, Cos 78, Procos in
    Italy 77, Cens 65) 3, 10, 11, 14, 15, 16, 17, 23
C. Cornelius CETHEGUS 43, 44, 45
M. Tullius CICERO (Q 75, Aed Pl 69, Pr 66, Cos 63,
    Procos Cilicia 51-0, Greece & Italy 49-7) viii, 58, 97

        aedileship viii, 7
        barrister   6, 7, 18, 29, 31, 77
        candidature for cos 26, 27, 29-32, 38
        & Catiline 20, 25, 27-28, 32, 35-36, 38-41, 43-49, 50, 62
        & Civil War 78-83, 88-93
        on Clodius & Bona Dea 53, 54, 56, 58-62
        on Clodius & Milo 68-77
        cos   25-29, 32, 35-49
        on Cornelius 16-18
        on equites & courts 6-10
        exile 50, 62-68, 89
        & First Triumvirate 20-24, 50-57, 63, 78
        on Verres 6-10
Q. Tullius CICERO (Q 68?, Aed Pl 65, Pr urb 62, Procos
    Asia 61-58) 29, 63, 66, 68, 69, 71, 90
L. Cornelius CINNA (Cos 87-4) 45, 64, 90
Ap. CLAUDIUS Pulcher (Pr de repetundis 57, Promag
    Sardinia 56, Cos 54, Procos Cilicia 53-1, Cens 50,
    Procos Greece 49-8) 70

Ap. CLAUDIUS Pulcher 77
CLODIA   72
P. CLODIUS Pulcher (Q 61-0, Tr Pl 58, Aed Cur 56) 20, 50, 53,
    54, 56, 57, 58-65, 67, 68-77

C. CORNELIUS (Q by 71, Tr Pl 67) 11, 16-18, 31
Q. CORNIFICIUS (Tr Pl 69, Pr by 66) 45
C. COSCONIUS (Pr 63, Procos Further Spain 62)   55
C. Aurelius COTTA (pr by 78, Cos 75, Procos
    Cisalpine Gaul 74)   2

L. Aurelius COTTA (Pr 70, Cos 65, Cens 64) 17, 87
M. Licinius CRASSUS Dives (Pr 73?, Procos 72-1,
    Cos 70, Cens 65, Cos II 55, Procos Syria 54-3) 20, 25, 42,
    45, 50-57, 58, 62, 72, 73, 78

C. Scribonius CURIO (Tr Pl 90, Pr by 80, Cos 76,
    Procos Macedonia (75-2) 3
C. Scribonius CURIO (Q 54 or 53?, Tr Pl suff 50,
    Propr 49) 52, 54, 59, 60, 72, 73, 79, 80

L. DOMITIUS Ahenobarbus (Q 66, Aed Cur 61, Pr 58,
    Cos 54, Procos Transalpine Gaul 49, in Greece
    49-8) 76, 79, 80, 87, 91
C. FABIUS (Tr Pl 55?, Legate Gaul 54-49) 91
Q. FABIUS Maximus (Aed Cur 57, Pr? by 48, Cos suff 45) 97
Q. FABRICIUS (Tr Pl 57) 63, 65
M. FAVONIUS (Q before 59, Aed 52, Pr 49) 59, 68, 72, 74

L. Valerius FLACCUS (Q 71 or 70, Pr 63, Propr
    Asia 62) 43, 44
Q. FUFIUS Calenus (Tr Pl 61, Pr 59, Cos 47, Promag
    Italy & Transalpine Gaul 42-0) 52, 59, 60, 61
L. FURIUS Philus (cos 136) 55
A. GABINIUS (Tr Pl 67, Pr by 61, Cos 58, Procos
    Syria 57-4) 11, 12, 13, 14

P. GABINIUS Capito 43, 44, 45
Q. GALLIUS (Aed Pl 67, Pr de maiestate 65) 18, 31

M' Acilius GLABRIO (Pr de repetundis 70, Cos 67,
    Procos Bithynia & Pontus 66) 9
P. Servilius GLOBULUS (Tr Pl 67, Pr 64, Propr Asia 63) 18
C. Sempronius GRACCHUS (Tr Pl 123/2) 22, 23, 24, 62, 87

Ti. Sempronius GRACCHUS (Tr Pl 133) 23, 24, 87
Q. HORTENSIUS (Aed 75, Pr de repetundis 72, Cos 69) 6, 7, 8,
    11, 12, 17, 59, 60, 61
C. LAELIUS Sapiens (Cos 140) 55
L. Cornelius LENTULUS Crus (Pr 58, Cos 49, Procos 48) 83, 84, 85
P. Cornelius LENTULUS Spinther (Q ca 74, Aed Cur 63,
    Pr 60, Promag Nearer Spain 59, Cos 57, Procos
    Cilicia 56-4) 45, 71, 73

P. Cornelius LENTULUS Sura (Q 81, Pr de repetundis 74,
    Cos 71, Pr II 63) 43, 44, 45, 47
M' Aemilius LEPIDUS (Proq by 78, Pr by 69, Cos 66) 16, 17

L. Licinius LUCULLUS (Q 87, Proq Greece 86, Asia
    85-0, Aed Cur 79, Pr 78, Promag Africa 77-6,
    Cos Cilicia 74, Procos Cilicia 73-68, Asia 73-69,
    Bithynia & Pontus 73-67) 60

M. Terentius Varro LUCULLUS (Q 83, Propr in
        Cispadane Gaul 82, Aed Cur 79, Pr 76, Cos 73,
        Procos Macedonia & Thrace 72-1)   17

C. Licinius MACER (Tr Pl 73, Pr 68?)   1-5
MAMERCUS Aemilius Lepidus Livianus (Pr by 81, Cos 77) 3
C. MANILIUS (Tr Pl 66) 11, 17
C. MANLIUS 39
Cn Cornelius Lentulus MARCELLINUS (Q 74?, Pr 60,
        Promag Syria 59-8, Cos 56)   70
C. Claudius MARCELLUS (Aed Cur? 56, Pr by 53, Cos 50) 70,79
C. Claudius MARCELLUS (Aed Cur? 56?, Pr by 52,
        Cos 49, Procos in Pompeian fleet 48)   86
M. Claudius MARCELLUS (Q 64, Aed Cur? 56, Pr by 54,
        Cos 51) 71, 76, 79, 80, 84, 89

C. MARIUS (Cos 107) 15, 48
M. Valerius MESSALLA Niger (Q ca 73, Pr by 64, Cos
        61, Cens 55) 59, 60, 67

C. MESSIUS (Tr Pl 57, Aed Pl 55) 67, 68
Q. Caecilius METELLUS Nepos (Tr Pl 62, Pr 60,
        Cos 57, Procos Nearer Spain 56-5) 14, 70
Q. Caecilius METELLUS Numidicus (Cos 109) 22, 61
Q. Caecilius METELLUS Pius (Pr 89, Procos 88-2,
        Cos 80, Procos Further Spain 79-1, Pont Max
        81-63) 17
Q. Caecilius METELLUS Pius Scipio Nasica (Tr Pl 59,
        Aed Cur 57?, Pr 55, Interrex 53, Cos 52, Procos
        Syria 49-8, Africa 48-6) 79, 80, 84, 85, 86

T. Annius MILO (Tr Pl 57, Pr 55) 58, 63, 68, 69, 70, 71, 72, 73-77
Mucius - see SCAEVOLA
T. MUNATIUS Plancus Byrsa (Tr Pl 52) 72
L. Licinius MURENA (Q 74, Pr urb 65, Procos Cisalpine
        & Transalpine Gaul 64-3, Cos 62) 32-34, 35
Cn. OCTAVIUS (Cos 87)   64
C. Vibius PANSA Caetronianus (Tr Pl 51, Aed? 49,
        Pr 48?, Promag Bithynia & Pontus 47-6,
        Cisalpine Gaul 45-4, Cos 43)   80
L. Aemilius PAULUS Lepidus (Q 59, Aed Cur? 55,
        Pr 53, Cos 50) 73, 79

L. Aemilius PAULUS Macedonicus (Cos 182) 48
L. Marcius PHILIPPUS (Cos 91)   15, 90
L. Marcius PHILIPPUS (Pr 62, Promag Syria 61-0,
        Cos 56)   87

L. Marcius PHILIPPUS (Tr Pl 49, Pr 44, Cos Suff 38)
      Procos Spain 34-3) 86
C. Calpurnius PISO (Pr by 70, Cos 67, Procos Cisalpine
      & Transalpine Gaul 66-5) 60
L. Calpurnius PISO Caesoninus (Q ca 70, Aed 64?, Pr by
      61, Cos 58, Procos Macedonia 57-5, Cens 50) 60, 85
M. Pupius PISO Frugi Calpurnianus (Q 83, Pr 72, Procos
      Spain 71, Cos 61) 59, 60

Cn. POMPEIUS Magnus (Propr Italy 83-2, Sicily 82-0,
      Africa 80-79, against Lepidus 77, Procos Nearer
      Spain 77-1, Cos 70, Procos against Pirates 67,
      against Mithridates 66-1, cura annonae 57-2,
      Cos II 55, Procos Spain 54-49, Cos III 52,
      Procos against Caesar 49-8) 4, 5, 6, 15, 16, 18, 20, 35, 48

      & the Civil War 78-93, 94
      & First Triumvirate 20, 50-57, 78
      against Pirates & Mithridates 11-16, 42
      in politics in Rome in 50's 20, 58, 59, 63, 67-68, 71-73,
         76, 78
      in Spain against Sertorius 4, 15
      & tribunate 4, 10, 11-18, 42

C. POMPTINUS (Pr 63, Promag Transalpine Gaul 62-59,
      Italy 59-4) 43, 44

L. QUINCTIUS (Tr Pl 74, Pr 68) 81
C. RABIRIUS viii, 35, 63
L. ROSCIUS Fabatus (Tr Pl 55?, Pr 49) 85
P. Servilius RULLUS (Tr Pl 63) 25, 29, 35
C. SALLUSTIUS Crispus (Q 55?, Tr Pl 52, Pr 46, Procos
      New Africa 46-5) 1, 35
L. Appuleius SATURNINUS (Tr Pl 103) 22, 24, 87
Q. Mucius SCAEVOLA (the Pontifex) (Cos 95) 90
M. Aemilius SCAURUS (Cos 115) 22
M. Aemilius SCAURUS (Q 66?, Proq Syria 65-4, Proq
      propr Syria 63-1, Aed Cur 58, Pr de vi 56,
      Promag Sardinia 55) 22
P. Cornelius SCIPIO Africanus (Cos 205) 48
P. Cornelius SCIPIO Africanus Aemilianus (Cos 147) 15, 48, 72
C. SEPTIMIUS (Pr 57, Procos Asia 56) 79, 80
Q. SERTORIUS (Q 90, Pr 83, Promag 82-73) 4
P. SERVILIUS Vatia Isauricus (Q by 60, Pr 54, Cos 48,
      Propr & Procos Asia 46-4, Cos II 41) 72

P. SESTIUS (Q 63, Proq Macedonia 62-1, Tr Pl 57, Pr ?,
    Promag Cilicia 49-8) 20-24, 58, 63-65

L. SICINIUS (Tr Pl 76) 2

D. Iunius SILANUS (Aed by 70, Pr by 67, Cos 62) 36, 45, 46, 47

L. STATILIUS 43, 44, 45

Faustus Cornelius SULLA (Q 54, Proq propr 49-7,
    Promag Africa 46) 86, 91

L. Cornelius SULLA Felix (Q 107, Proq 106-5, propr
    105, Pr urb 93, Propr Cilicia 92, Cos 88, Procos
    Greece, Macedonia, Asia 87-4, Italy 83-1, Dict 82-79,
    (Cos II 80)   vi, vii, viii, ix, 1, 2, 3, 6, 36, 39, 40, 41, 42,
    45, 85, 86, 87, 92, 94

P. Cornelius SULLA (pr by 68, Cos desig 65) 69, 70

Ser. Cornelius SULLA   45

Ser. SULPICIUS Rufus (Q 74, Pr de peculatu 65, Inter-
    rex 52, Cos 51) 32-34, 79

L. Manlius TORQUATUS (Proq 84-1, Pr 68?, Procos
    Asia? 67?, Cos 65, Procos Macedonia 64-3) 17

C. TREBONIUS (Q 60?, Tr Pl 55, Pr urb 48, Procos
    Further Spain 47-6, Cos suff 45, Procos Asia 44-3) 91

Q. VARIUS Severus Hibrida (Tr Pl 90) 22

M. Terentius VARRO (Q 85?, Tr Pl?, Pr?, Official
    Librarian 45) 57, 96

C. VERRES (Q 84, Proq 83, Pr urb 74, Propr Sicily
    73-1) viii, 6-10

L. VILLIUS Annalis (Pr by 58) 79, 80

L. VOLCACIUS Tullus (Pr by 69, Cos 66) 16

T. VOLTURCIUS   43, 44

b) Laws & Proposals

lex Acilia (122) 6

lex Appuleia agraria (100) 22

lex Aurelia de tribunicia potestate (75) 2

lex Aurelia iudiciaria (70) ix

lex Calpurnia de rebus repetundis (149) viii, 6

lex Cassia tabellaria (137) 23

lex Cornelia de maiestate (81) 16, 17

lex decem tribunorum (52) 82, 89

lex Gabinia de piratis (67) 11, 12, 13

lex Iulia agraria (59) & de agro Campano (59) vi, 50, 53, 55, 58

lex Iulia sumptuaria (49-4) 96

lex Licinia et Aebutia (mid C2) 11

c) Miscellaneous

Terms marked with an asterisk are explained in the
Glossary.

Latin words listed in brackets in this index appear in
translation in the text.

LACTORS

London Association of Classical Teachers — Original Records: a series of translations of sources for Ancient History.

LACTORs already published:

Copies of all LACTORs may be obtained post free in U.K. —

From
LACT Publications Secretary,
5 Normington Close,
Leigham Court Road,
London SW16 2QS

or by JACT members from:
Dr. James Roy,
The Department of Ancient
History and Archaeology,
The University,
Sheffield S10 2TN.